THE SECOND
Food &
DRINK
BOOK

THE SECOND FOOD & DRINK BOOK

MICHAEL BARRY · JILL GOOLDEN · CHRIS KELLY

BBC PUBLICATIONS

Published by BBC Publications
A division of BBC Enterprises Ltd
35 Marylebone High St, London W1M 4AA

First published 1986
© Michael Barry, Jill Goolden and Chris Kelly 1986

ISBN 0 563 20529 6

Typeset by Belmont Press, Northampton
Printed in Great Britain by Redwood Burn, Wiltshire

Design: Annette Peppis
Cover illustration: Ashley Hamilton Lloyd
Inside illustrations: Mikki Rain

CONTENTS

INTRODUCTION 7

STARTERS 9

FISH 19

CHICKEN 1 33

CHICKEN 2 40

MEAT 48

EXOTIC VEGETABLES 58

PUDDINGS 70

BREAD BASKET 83

CHEESE AND CHUTNEY 92

CHRISTMAS 99

INTRODUCTION TO WINE 115

WHAT IS WINE? 120

THE LANGUAGE OF WINE EXPLAINED 128

HOW MUCH SHOULD YOU PAY? 142

A-Z OF WINES 145

SERVING WINE – A FEW SIMPLE RULES 161

INDEX 167

INTRODUCTION

This, the second *Food and Drink* book, is much fatter than the first. Once again, at the heart of it is a large collection of appetising, practical and easy-to-make recipes. This time, however, there is a comprehensive guide for wine-buyers (with the emphasis on what's available for under £3 a bottle). There's also a wide range of background information about traditional, additive-free British foodstuffs and where to get them. There's an introduction to the glories of British farmhouse cheeses, for instance, an early morning visit to Billingsgate, and news of a great comeback being staged by some tasty breeds of pig.

In essence, this book is about alternatives. It is, of course, convenient to buy everything you need in supermarkets (and they're taking their responsibilities to the consumer increasingly seriously: in the last 12 months they've made progress on a broad front, with many instances of the removal of additives and a greater frankness in labelling). These are developments we obviously applaud. At the same time, however, the demands of the mass market have tended to spawn products which are reasonably priced and good-looking but often woefully lacking in flavour and variety. Tomatoes, cheese and pork are just three examples we investigate here. One of the messages of this book is: 'flavour lives' – and we'll tell you where.

That's a war cry often heard on *Food and Drink*, which, on the strength of the 1985-6 series, has established itself as the most popular such programme ever shown on BBC 2. You don't need to have seen it to enjoy the book, but if you have, you'll note that what follows has a familiar pattern.

I introduce each chapter with information about the foods involved. The recipes themselves are provided and commented upon by Michael Barry, our resident crafty cook. The guide to buying, keeping and enjoying wines (at prices guaranteed not to bankrupt you) is the work of our drinks expert, Jill Goolden. Jill also provides general recommendations for each chapter of recipes, such as which type of wine goes best with a particular kind of food.

As they say in Ireland, in a somewhat ambiguous but beautiful toast, 'may the road rise up to meet you'.

STARTERS

The art of the starter, according to Anton Mosimann of the Dorchester, is to make sure that it's light, appealing, colourful, fresh and not overpowering in taste. As a general rule, he recommends salads, poached fish or soup. It was the first of the three that another fine chef, Michael Quinn, chose when he accepted a *Food and Drink* challenge in the North of England. Michael, who used to be Chef de Cuisine at the Ritz, now cooks at the Ettington Park Hotel near Stratford-Upon-Avon. He agreed to take a day off from the well-equipped kitchens where he presides over a team of 30, and make lunch for the 300 patients of Lodge Moor Hospital in Sheffield. The task, daunting enough in itself, began to look positively Himalayan as Michael was told about 'certain limitations'. Clearly the meal would have to be made from nutritious ingredients, that much he expected; but the tight budget of just 50p a head didn't leave him much room for flourishes and, worst of all, the food would have to be loaded into container-trolleys by 11 am. There it would sit, slowly surrendering its life-juices, for anything up to two hours before being served to the diners, who, of course, would rather not be there in the first place.

Despite the immense willingness of the kitchen staff, things didn't quite turn out as planned. The attractive prototype Michael made for the main course (lamb on a bed of pulses surrounded by vegetables) could have been an illustration from *À La Carte* magazine, but on the production line it managed to resemble muddy gravel strewn with seaweed. Fortunately, this didn't mar the nutritional value of the dish, and the hospital is to adopt it as a regular feature on the menu.

The valiant Michael Quinn's experience should console any amateur cook faced with a crisis; just think, however bad it seems, it could be much worse! As I mentioned, the chef's starter on that memorable occasion was a salad (see page 15 for the recipe). There were reservations about the quails' eggs from patients who'd never tried them, but otherwise it went down well. As an occasional treat, quails'eggs are both pretty and delicious. Now available at supermarkets, they're relatively expensive (around 13p each) but you don't need many to make a plate of crudités or a salad look special.

Hens' eggs, too, are versatile allies when you're under starter's orders, and for those concerned with the life-style of the layers, a short guide to the various EEC classifications might be useful. The vast majority of eggs sold are still battery-produced, but they might be described in a number of ways, including 'fresh' or 'newly laid'. Now, new phrases are appearing on egg boxes:

Deep Litter: The birds are kept in units with litter on the floor. They're not caged as battery hens are, and there must be no more than seven hens per square metre.

Perchery or Barn: The hens are kept in similar units to those in Deep Litter, except they also have perches. Can cost about 15p a dozen more than ordinary battery-produced eggs.

Free-range: The hens must have continuous daytime access to open-air runs. The ground should be mainly covered with vegetation and the maximum number of hens per hectare (2.2 acres) is 1000. Can cost up to 40p a dozen more than battery.

Semi-intensive: The conditions are the same as for Free-range except that the maximum number of chickens per hectare is rather greater at 4000.

Given our climate, one of the great starter mysteries in the UK is our neglect of soup. It's nourishing, easy to make, economical and full of variety, and yet it's still often underrated. This disregard is reflected to a great extent in the amount of top-selling tinned, packet and instant soups on the market.

In tests of ready-made soups carried out by Home Economics students from the Polytechnic of North London, canned soups were preferred for texture, flavour and appearance, although in general they are slightly more expensive per portion than the packet or instant soups. The three the students liked best were Crosse & Blackwell Cream of Chicken, Heinz Cream of Tomato and Heinz Cream of Chicken, although it's worth bearing in mind that soups described as 'Cream of . . . ' are marginally higher in fat. In the packet range, the only product that was rated anything other than poor or very poor was Crosse & Blackwell Bonne Cuisine Cream of Chicken. Among the instant soups, where the brand leaders are Batchelors, Knorr and Heinz, all the flavours tested (vegetable, tomato and chicken) got the thumbs down. All in all, it's well worth making your own, especially with Michael's recipes which are simple *and* delicious. Read on . . . .

PUMPKIN SOUP (FONDO DEL SOL)
Serves 4-6

This is a wonderful soup for the autumn: rich, golden and warming, and named after 'the heart of the sun' in its native South America. You can make it any time you buy a whole pumpkin, but it's particularly fun if you buy one around Halloween and, having scraped the flesh out for the soup, carefully use the shell as a serving tureen before turning it into a lantern. (Be careful not to get the shell too thin!) To prepare the pumpkin (which should probably weigh around 2 pounds, or 900 grams, to start with), discard all the seeds and the soft pulp around them, peel and chop. (If you haven't got a blender, grate all the vegetables.) Croûtons are great with this (see page 89).

1 tbspn of oil (preferably peanut)
1 clove garlic, chopped
1½ lb (700g) prepared pumpkin
8 oz (225g) tomatoes, chopped
8 oz (225g) onions, chopped
3-4 tspns of tomato purée
1-1½ pints (900ml) of water or vegetable stock

Heat the oil in a saucepan and add the garlic. Then add the pumpkin, tomatoes and onions. Mix in the tomato purée and stir the ingredients over a low heat for 3-4 minutes.

Add the water or stock carefully: the consistency should be like single cream. Simmer for 30 minutes and then purée the mixture in a food processor or liquidiser. Re-heat and serve in either a hollowed-out pumpkin or a tureen.

FRENCH VEGETABLE SOUP
Serves 4

A classic *potage aux legumes* as featured in countless French bistros and homes. The formula is simple but perfect: fresh ingredients mixed in the right proportions, cooked in the classic way and served without delay, and it results in one of the great soups of all time. You can use the same principles for a number of different vegetables, but do use fresh and not already-cooked ones, and never add more than two vivid flavours together or you may find they cancel each other out. (Parsnip and walnut are two that go well together, as are jerusalem artichoke and spring onion.) Sprinkle with chopped parsley and serve with wholemeal bread.

1 tbspn butter
8 oz (225g) leeks, chopped and well washed
8 oz (225g) potatoes, peeled and chopped
8 oz (225g) carrots, peeled and chopped
Salt and freshly ground black pepper
1½-2 pints (roughly 1 litre) of water or vegetable stock

Melt butter in a pan and add the leeks, potatoes and carrots. Stir for 2-3 minutes until all the vegetables are well coated in butter. Add the water or stock, season and simmer for 20 minutes.

Pour the contents into a food processor or liquidiser and mix until blended but still reasonably chunky. (This soup can be eaten without liquidising.)

TOMATO AND ORANGE SOUP
Serves 4

A modern soup with a rich yet sharp taste, this makes use of one of the new products that the latest techniques have given us: passata – a light purée of Italian tomatoes, sieved and pasturised with nothing added but a pinch of salt. Additive-free, it provides that rich tomato flavour and colour that are so often missing in English tomatoes. Passata is becoming more available – a growing number of supermarkets stock it at certain times of the year. For Cream of Tomato, just add 2 table-spoons of double cream or yoghurt.

1 tbspn olive oil
1 onion, finely chopped
Juice and grated rind of an orange
1 × 1¾ pint (1 litre) bottle passata
10 fl oz (275ml) water
Salt and freshly ground black pepper
Cubed tomato to garnish

Heat the oil in a deep pan and add the onion. Cook until translucent and then add rind and juice of orange and stir thoroughly. Add the passata and water and bring to the boil. Simmer for not more than 5 minutes. Season to taste and garnish with cubed tomato. This makes a delicious thick soup, but if you prefer you can add more water to thin it down.

RAINBOW STUFFED EGGS

Serves 4

Both pretty and pretty simple to do. A lovely starter for a family meal or a dinner party, these multi-coloured eggs are also good for a buffet or reception. While I've suggested three flavour/colour combinations, you can ring the changes to suit your own tastes and what's available in the garden or larder. Do fill the eggs carefully: the simpler the dish, the more appearance matters. The method for hard-boiling the eggs is worth noting too: it avoids grey yolks and dark rings, which is a good idea even if they are just for a picnic.

6 eggs (Free-range or Perchery if possible)
6 tspns real mayonnaise

1 tspn tomato purée
½ tspn dried basil
Salt and freshly ground black pepper

4 anchovy fillets, chopped
1 tspn parsley, finely chopped

1 tspn mango chutney
½ level tspn curry powder
Salt and freshly ground black pepper

Put the eggs in cold water, bring to the boil and simmer for 10 minutes. Run under cold water; crack the shells and peel when cool. Halve each egg lengthways and remove yolks. Divide yolks into three bowls and mix 2 tablespoons of mayonnaise into each. Then add one of the flavour/colour combinations to each bowl. (Tomato for red; parsley for green; curry for yellow.) Mix thoroughly and then fill four egg halves with each colour, moulding the mixture up to a peak. Serve each person one half-egg of each colour.

Jill's wine recommendations:
Eggs can tend to coat the mouth and so diminish the enjoyment of the subtleties of fine wine. A good excuse to serve cheap plonk with eggs! Red is best; preferably something robust such as a vin de pays or VDQS from southern France.

Michael Quinn's Quails' Egg Salad and Soup

As Chris wrote at the beginning of this chapter, Michael Quinn took on the job of cooking for 300 hospital patients. His recipes were incredibly varied considering the miniscule budget he had to work with. Two suggestions used quails' eggs, which are now widely available. These are my versions of Michael's ingenious ideas.

Quails' egg salad
Serves 4

8 quails' eggs
2 ozs (50g) smoked salmon
3 varieties of lettuce (oak leaf, radicchio and endive are best)
For the dressing:
4 tbspns olive oil
2 tbspns lemon juice
Pinch each sugar and salt

Hard boil the eggs for 3 minutes, shell and halve when cool. Cut the salmon into strips, ¼ inch (0.5cm) wide. Wash and shred the lettuces and arrange pieces of each one on four plates. Place the eggs on the lettuce and sprinkle with the salmon strips. Shake the oil, lemon juice, sugar and salt into a dressing mixture and pour over just before serving.

Quails' egg soup
Serves 4

2 pints (1.1 litres) chicken stock (see page 39 for method)
½ leek, finely shredded
1 carrot, grated
4 quails' eggs (raw)

Bring the stock to the boil, add the vegetables and simmer for 2 minutes. Pour into individual bowls. Crack the eggs and add one to each bowl. Leave to poach for 2 minutes and serve.

ONION BHAJI
Serves 4

This home-made version of an Indian restaurant favourite is really easy to make and incredibly 'moreish'. If you serve it before an Indian meal it becomes additionally exotic served with prawn chutney *(balichow)* and plain yoghurt. I also find it great for a snack at tea-time and especially popular with my children. The less usual ingredients – chick-pea flour and prawn *balichow* – can be found in oriental food shops. They are worth seeking out.

6 oz (175g) chick-pea flour (called 'besan')
1 tspn oil
1 Spanish onion, thinly sliced
1 tspn fresh coriander (or parsley, finely chopped)
10 fl oz (275ml) water (approx)
For the topping:
Prawn *balichow*
Plain yoghurt

Mix all the ingredients together except the onion. The mixture should have the consistency of double cream: if not, carefully add more water. Mix in the onion slices and stand for half an hour. Heat a big frying-pan. Grease it lightly and drop tablespoons of the mixture onto it. Cook on a high heat for about 1½ minutes each side, pressing down with a spatula. When cooked spread each Bhaji with half a teaspoon of prawn chutney and then top with a teaspoon of plain yoghurt.

PEAR AND STILTON STARTER
Serves 4

The combination of pear, walnuts and Stilton cheese is more usual at the end of a meal, but I think it makes a spectacular starter.

This recipe uses an apple cutter that divides apples or pears into 12 sections while cutting out the core. It was available in most kitchen shops until I demonstrated it on television – then most of them seemed to disappear overnight!

Fromage frais, by the way, is a French version of cottage cheese made from fermented skimmed milk. It's delicious, creamy, low in fat and available in a number of supermarkets.

4 oz (110g) Stilton cheese
4 oz (110g) fromage frais (or cottage cheese)
2 oz (50g) walnuts, shelled
4 ripe Comice pears
Lemon juice

Cream the cheese and fromage frais together until the mixture is smooth. Chop and add all but four walnut halves. Divide the cheese mixture into four and place in the middle of four saucers. Peel and segment the pears into 12 pieces. Dip into water with some lemon juice to stop them browning. Press the pear sections into the cheese, re-creating the shape of the pear and top each with a walnut half. Serve within half an hour.

Avocado milkshake

Serves 4

Not so much a starter as an exotic addition to a weekend lunch. Made by the jugful, it's an easily drunk first course to a garden buffet. Either way, this adult milkshake is extra good for you if you use semi-skimmed milk, as well as having a most refreshing flavour combined with a rich texture. Do use *ripe* avocados or you'll never know true happiness.

10 fl oz (150ml) of semi-skimmed fresh milk
½ avocado, very ripe
1 cupful pineapple chunks (fresh, or canned but unsweetened)
1 dspn runny honey
1 small carton low-fat natural yoghurt
Cup of ice cubes
Pinch of salt

Blend all the ingredients until thick and frothy.

NB. Some blenders cannot cope with ice cubes: make sure yours can, or use a food processor.

FISH

In the UK, we eat more fish than any other country in Europe except Sweden. We consume around 370,000 tons a year, most of it in the form of fish products from the freezer, such as fish cakes, cod in sauce, fish fingers, scampi fries and the rest.

So far, so good. But it's been estimated that around £6,000,000 worth of what we buy annually as fish is in fact water. We are the only nation in the world which allows glazed prawns to be sold by gross weight and in some cases they've been found to contain up to 40% added water, although the recommended guidelines suggest 12 to 15% as being reasonable. The UK Association of Frozen Food Producers have 'urged Ministers to introduce legislation at the earliest opportunity requiring that the actual weight of fish, net of glaze, be declared'. And not before time. Meanwhile, however, a number of companies are voluntarily specifying net weight on their packaging; if you want to know what you're getting for your money, they're the ones to buy from, so look out for them.

David Walker of the Shropshire Trading Standards Department raised the issue of water at fish prices in his submission to the Advisory Committee of the Ministry of Agriculture, Fisheries and Food. His report makes fairly depressing reading. As well as highlighting double-glazing in prawns, it tackled the composition of fish fingers. Introduced in the US during the 1950s as a breadcrumb-coated strip of fillet, this great family favourite used to consist of 80% fish and 20% crumbs, but not any more. Now the average proportion is only 56% fish – the lowest count Walker found was 34%.

The composition of the fish content also came in for analysis. Many brands include a proportion of minced fish, which, although nutritionally fine, contains more water than unminced, and is an inferior product with a quite different colour and texture. Minced fish is also to be found sheltering under the breadcrumbs (or batter) of certain types of cod portions, and even in examples of breaded scampi. Pending changes in the laws on labelling, the buyer unequipped with X-ray eyes is at a considerable disadvantage. The sooner we're told exactly what's in the fish products we buy, and in what quantities, the better. Until then, look for the products which offer the clearest information. Waitrose and Sainsbury's, for example, do specify which of their fish fingers are made from minced fish and which from unminced fillet. If in doubt elsewhere, ask.

Perhaps the saddest part of the story is that of the 5 ounces (150g) of fish we average weekly per person, only 1 ounce (25g) is fresh.

Thirty years ago there were 9000 retail outlets for fish in the UK; now that figure is down by two-thirds. Since the Second World War our fishing fleet has shrunk dramatically. Among the reasons for the decline were: the growth in the number of women working outside the home, who value the convenience of frozen fish; the relentless rise of high street rents; and the fact that we've tended to view fresh fish as a change rather than as a real alternative to meat. In the last few years, however, there's been evidence of a revival of interest in fresh fish. Its fat, unlike that of meat, is now thought to be good for us, helping to prevent heart attacks and possibly rheumatoid arthritis. Farmed fish (trout and salmon) is available all year round, too, and the increasing availability of different ethnic foods opens up new avenues in adventurous fish cooking. No longer entirely satisfied with the frozen product, which is undeniably convenient but equally undeniably bland, we're once more on the look-out for the real thing. Supermarket chains have taken note and many branches offer a gratifyingly wide range of fresh fish.

Frank Lincoln, now retired after more than half a century in the fresh fish trade, is delighted by the comeback. When he joined his father in the family's Southall shop during the Depression (selling wet fish as well as fish and chips), the standard order was 'a twopenny and one'.

Frank generously offered to give me a few tips at Billingsgate market: he loves both the place and all the people in it. Nevertheless, at 7 o'clock on a winter's morning, it's no location for a sensitive soul (or even a sensitive sole). The misty chill seeps in from London's dockland and the wet floor quick-freezes your feet, but to listen to the sparky good humour of the white-coated buyers and sellers, you'd think it was the height of summer. Porters with barrows bear directly down on you, too busy to make a detour; 'they take no prisoners', says Frank. As we pass between the dead, gleaming shoals he recites the fishy litany: there are pike and pout whiting; ray and big plump scallops; rainbow trout and mock halibut ('it's a bastard – like some old customers I used to know!'); oysters and grey mullet; bloaters, brill and bass; lovely Scottish salmon with the bloom still on them, and many more. Thirty per cent of the fish sold at Billingsgate is imported, much of it fresh, which accounts for the choice of exotics, including bourgeois (from the Seychelles), black-and-gold mirror carp, and freshwater bream.

The only part of Billingsgate that doesn't offer fish is the small café ('we couldn't give it away!'). Over a good strong cuppa and a bacon sandwich, Frank tells me what to watch out for when you're buying fresh fish. The skin should have a gloss which you can't rub off; if the head's attached, make sure the eyes are bright and the gills are red rather than brown. If it's cod you're after, on the fresh fillets you can distinctly make out the individual flakes of flesh, rather like the rings of a tree. The skin of fresh fish is smooth and slimy to the touch, whereas the skin of frozen fish is rough.

Frank Lincoln reckons fresh fish is a must for fish and chips, not just because it tastes much better but also because it absorbs less fat than frozen fillets and is therefore more economical. He favours ground-nut oil for frying and Maris Piper potatoes for the chips.

One of the most sought-after items in the market the morning we were there was monkfish, although it goes by plenty of other names. Some people have called it angler fish, but technically the monkfish (squatina squatina) is not the same as the angler fish (lophius piscatorius). In France it's known as lotte, and even Alan Davidson's superb book *North Atlantic Seafood* offers no theories as to why, in Scotland, it's called Molly Gowan. Whichever label you put on it (and despite the fact that it looks frightening enough to haunt houses), monkfish, with its succulent, white flesh, makes wonderful eating.

The variety available wholesale at Billingsgate is increasingly working its way through to shops and restaurants. Thanks to enthusiasts like Frank Lincoln, who've encouraged us to settle for nothing but the best, we're once again recognising the versatility of fresh fish.

MONKFISH

Despite the controversy over what it's called, Monkfish is one of the great fish delicacies. With its firm, almost boneless flesh it's easy to prepare and will convert all but the most ardent fish haters.

Here are two recipes which treat it in a similar way to meat – kebabed or sautéed in a spicy sauce. Both are 'special occasion' dishes, and both taste particularly good accompanied by rice.

MONKFISH KEBABS
Serves 4

This uses the flavourings of the eastern Mediterranean for taste and the colours of South American peppers for decoration. It's a great combination. Use either flat-sided or wooden skewers: they make it much easier to turn the fish. Serve on a bed of long-grain rice.

1½ lbs (700g) monkfish, skinned and cubed
1 onion
3 peppers (red, yellow, green, ideally)
For the marinade:
½ cup olive oil
½ cup lemon juice
1 tbspn green leaves of fennel, chopped
1 clove garlic, crushed

Put the oil, lemon juice, fennel and crushed garlic into a large bowl and stir together. Place the cubed monkfish in the bowl and leave to marinate for 2-6 hours.

Slice the onion and peppers into 1-inch (2.5cm) squares and thread alternate slices of the vegetables and cubes of monkfish onto flat skewers. Cook for 5 minutes on each side under a hot grill, brushing with the marinade.

MONKFISH IN GREEN PEPPERCORN SAUCE

Serves 4

Green peppercorn sauce has become a 'nouvelle' standard in recent years. It usually accompanies meat or poultry; fish is normally so delicate a taste it tends to be overwhelmed by the spicy unripe peppercorns. Monkfish is the notable exception, with its firm texture and distinctive character.

Cut the fish into noisette shapes if you can – little roundels like the heart of lamb chops.

1 tspn butter
4 fl oz (100ml) water or fish stock
1½ lbs (700g) monkfish fillets
1 bay leaf
8 oz (225g) double cream
2 tspns green peppercorns (in brine)
Salt to taste

Melt the butter in the water or stock. Cut the fish into ½ inch (1cm) nuggets across the grain of the fillet. Poach gently for 10 minutes in the water with the bay leaf. Remove the fish and keep warm. Add the cream and peppercorns to the pan. Bring to the boil, turn down low and add the fish for 1 minute. Salt and serve with the fish nuggets placed cleanly on top of the sauce.

HERRINGS IN OATMEAL
Serves 4

After a ban of several years on most herring fishing, the fleets are out once more. That's the good news. The bad news is that many of us seem to have lost the habit of eating them. Let's get into the habit again – herring is both cheap and nutritious.

In Scotland, this recipe has practically become the national fish dish. Apart from its superb eating qualities, it's extra healthy because it's low in fat (except for fish oil, but even that is good for you, we now believe) and contains fibre from the oatmeal. Don't season the fish – it'll be done already. Serve with lemon wedges on warm plates with brown bread and butter.

4 herrings, cleaned
4 tbspns oatmeal or porridge oats
1 tbspn salt

Heat a solid frying-pan with the salt sprinkled in. When the salt starts to change colour, carefully add the fish. Let them cook for 3 minutes. Turn, lower the heat and cook for another 5 minutes. Sprinkle the oatmeal onto the herring. Turn the heat up high and shake until the oatmeal starts to brown and the herrings are crispy.

SWEET-AND-SOUR PRAWNS
Serves 4

This is a Cantonese recipe and, like many Chinese dishes, involves stir-frying. The principle is that a very hot pan seals in the flavour of the ingredients, and a brief stir-fry leaves vegetables crisp and crunchy rather than horribly soggy. The ideal instrument for stir-frying is the wok – often given as a Christmas present, but I fear just as often consigned to the cupboard. Get it out and give it a try! If you do not yet possess one, there are a number to choose from at varying prices. The type I recommend has a long handle and a *flat* bottom, making it ideal for use on western stoves. Prices range from £5 to £15 (for the flat-bottomed woks). One other piece of advice: follow the instructions carefully for seasoning your wok before you cook with it.

Most Chinese don't eat sweet-and-sour dishes in their own meals nearly as much as we do in Chinese restaurants, but in the Cantonese cooking from the South of China, you do often find fruit and savoury ingredients used in conjunction. Cooked with brightly coloured peppers, prawns make a quick and savoury complement to the sharp, sweet sauce. (Don't keep the prawns waiting once they're hot – they'll go rubbery.) Serve with plenty of rice.

1 tbspn oil
1 red pepper, finely chopped
1 green pepper, finely chopped
1 yellow pepper, finely chopped
3-4 spring onions, chopped
8 oz (225g) prawns, defrosted or fresh and peeled
Pinch of Five Spice powder (Chinese seasoning available from
    supermarkets)
1 tspn fresh ginger, finely chopped
1 clove garlic, finely chopped
For the sauce:
1 tbspn soy sauce
½ tbspn cornflour
1 tbspn brown sugar
1 tbspn cider vinegar
1 tbspn tomato purée

Mix the sauce ingredients together until they're smooth. Heat the oil (preferably in a wok, but a frying-pan will do). Add the vegetables and stir over a high heat for 2 minutes. Add the prawns, the Five Spice powder, the ginger and garlic: heat through briefly and then add the sauce. Stir in until the sauce goes shiny and thick and serve immediately.

LOUISIANA PRAWNS
Serves 4

In Louisiana they use the same basic ingredients that the Chinese use for Sweet-and-Sour Prawns, but the dish that emerges is very different in style and flavour. That's true even though the dish in Louisiana will also be served with rice. It makes an unusual and exotic main course, though in New Orleans it's often served as part of the extended breakfast they invented – 'brunch'. (Again, make sure the prawns don't have to sit about before being eaten.)

2 tbspns oil
8 oz (225g) each of red and green peppers,
    sliced in ½ inch (1cm) strips
8 oz (225g) onions, sliced
8 oz (225g) tinned tomatoes
½ tspn molasses (or brown sugar)
½ tspn chilli powder
1 lb (450g) prawns, defrosted

Sauté the peppers and onions in the oil for 5 minutes. Add the tomatoes, molasses and chilli powder. Simmer for 10 minutes, add the prawns, heat through and serve.

TROUT EN PAPILLOTE

Papillote (or 'envelope cooking') was developed to an art at the turn of the century. Originally it used real parchment and specially heated ovens: nowadays it's perfect for microwave cooking, particularly with fish recipes. See-through roaster bags make the perfect alternative to parchment, but keep the bag above the food and make sure you leave a steam hole or there could be a mess! Don't, whatever you do, use the wire seals provided with some bags: sparks would fly, literally. Although this recipe is for trout, any fish will cook well in the microwave using this technique. (You can, of course, use a conventional oven, but it's not as quick.)

Per person:
1 trout, cleaned
Salt and freshly ground black pepper
1 tbspn chopped dill (or tspn dried dill)
1 tspn butter
1 slice lemon

Lay the fish in a microwave-acceptable dish. Season and sprinkle with the dill. Place the butter and lemon on the fish. Place in roaster bag, make a steam hole and put into the microwave for 4-5 minutes (check your microwave's instructions for an exact time). If using a conventional oven, bake for 20 minutes at 375°F (190°C) or gas mark 5. When cooked, remove and leave to stand for 1 minute. Serve on warm plates.

Jill's wine recommendations:
Simple fish dishes are a magnificent foil for the drier, slightly acidic white wines such as those from Alsace in France, English wines and, adding a hint of a sparkle, the Portuguese vinho verde. The serving of white wine with fish is a tradition with a good reason behind it: red wines don't 'go', they give both the wine and the fish a metallic taste.

TROUT ALMONDINE

Serves 4

With fresh trout so widely available they make an attractive introduction to fish, especially as they are mercifully free of bones compared to most freshwater fish.

The combination of trout and almonds is a classic; this version doubles the almonds. Try serving it with steamed cucumber pieces tossed in a little butter.

4 tbspns ground almonds
4 trout, cleaned
2 tbspns oil
2 oz (50g) butter
4 tspns slivered almonds
2 tbspns lemon juice

Put the ground almonds into a bag and shake each trout in it, coating thoroughly. Heat the oil in a pan and place the trout in it. Sauté them gently for 5 minutes a side, remove and keep warm. Add the butter, turn up the heat and sauté the slivered almonds until they are just brown. Add the lemon juice and carefully pour over the trout. Serve at once on *hot* plates.

SALMON SASHIMI

Serves 2-4

Sashimi is the Japanese way of eating raw fish: delicate slices of salmon, tuna or whatever, dipped in spicy soy sauce and savoured. Before you turn your nose up, it's worth remembering that our smoked salmon is raw too (it's only flavoured, not cooked in the smoke), so it's worth giving this recipe a try as a light first course. It's not at all 'fishy' but delicate and subtle. It is also interesting that Japanese food like this was one of the main inspirations of nouvelle cuisine. When arranged prettily, it looks as good as it tastes.

8 oz (225g) fillet of salmon, as fresh as possible
4 radishes, grated
1 carrot, grated
4 tspns soy sauce (Japanese *shoyu*, if you can find it)
½ tspn mustard

Get your fishmonger to skin the salmon, or skin it yourself using salt to provide a grip on its skin. Remove *all* the bones and cut it across the grain into ¼ inch (0.5cm) slices, about the size of cigarette cards. Lay these out attractively and decorate with the carrots and radishes. To eat, each person mixes a smidgeon of mustard and a little soy sauce in their bowl, and dips a salmon piece covered with grated vegetable in the sauce.

New England Cod Chowder
Serves 4-6

Ever since the tavern scene in Moby Dick, New England Cod Chowder has been a legendary dish. There's even a famous peninsular in Boston named 'Cape Cod' and the rich, creamy fish stew that comes from there should be eaten, not just read about.

There are many recipes claiming to be authentic: this one is fairly authentic – if crafty – and very warming on a cold night.

1½ lb (700g) potatoes, in 1 inch (2.5cm) cubes
8 oz (225g) onions, in 1 inch (2.5cm) cubes
10 fl oz (275ml) water
1½ lb (700g) chunky cod fillet, skinned and cubed
1 pint (570ml) milk
1 tspn cornflour
Salt and freshly ground black pepper
8 water biscuits (or Ritz crackers)

Cook the potato and onion cubes in the water until almost tender. Add the fish and all but half a cup of milk. Simmer for 5 minutes. Mix the cornflour and remaining milk, season lightly and add to the stew. Simmer till it thickens and serve with the biscuits or crackers crumbled over the top.

Sweetcorn, green peppers, tomatoes and shrimps are all tasty additions, but then it isn't New England Cod Chowder!

Jill's wine recommendations:
The refreshingly high zing of acidity that stands up well to the more filling fish dishes is found in wines such as Sancerre, made from the Sauvignon grape. Austrian wines, too, are known for their slight tartness (and having emerged thoroughly chastened after the recent wine scandal, are now again a good bet – and frequently a very good buy).

BAKED OYSTERS

Serves 4

Oysters are making a comeback in the UK, but they are still expensive enough to make half a dozen each for dinner a strain on your bank balance.

In many countries, though, oysters are eaten cooked, which is not only helpful for the squeamish amongst us, it stretches them considerably. A dozen cooked like this will make a good starter for four people. The Gruyère, by the way, is essential: Cheddar won't do.

12 large oysters
5 fl oz (150ml) single cream
1 tspn cornflour
1 oz (25g) butter
4 drops Tabasco Sauce
4 oz (110g) Gruyère, grated
French bread

Discard the shallow halves of the oyster shells. Keeping the oysters in their 'deep' shells, stand them in a baking tray on a bed of salt deep enough to keep them stable. Make a sauce whisking the cream, cornflour and butter together over a low heat. When thick, flavour with the Tabasco and most of the cheese. Carefully spoon a coating of sauce over each oyster, sprinkle with the remaining cheese and bake at 450°F(230°C), gas mark 8 for 10 minutes. Serve immediately with the French bread, to mop up the sauce.

CHICKEN 1

According to the latest estimates, salmonella (the bacterium which causes food poisoning if not eliminated by careful cooking) can be found in 80% of frozen broiler chickens sold to the public. The birds may have eaten food contaminated with salmonella; they could have been infected in the crowded conditions of the broiler house; or the infection might have taken place at a later stage: in a poultry processing plant, where many thousands of birds are slaughtered and eviscerated every day. Whether there's an equally high incidence of salmonella among Free-range chickens, we simply don't know. Salmonella is by no means the only cause of food poisoning, but it does account for a significant proportion. In 1983, of all the food poisoning in England and Wales investigated by laboratories, 87% was due to salmonella. In 45% of the outbreaks in which the cause was found, poultry was the vehicle. In 1985 the Central Public Health Laboratory in London confirmed nearly 13,000 infections (nationwide) by salmonella, and it's thought that for every infection investigated by laboratories, there might be as many as 100 which go unreported and therefore untested. Although the graph tends to fluctuate a bit (for instance, there's been a very slight and rather puzzling drop in the last two years), there's been a steady rise in salmonella food poisoning since 1968, and more sharply since 1976.

So, eating, as we do, something like 1,000,000 chickens a week, it's bound to be a cause for concern. The consolation is that as long as we follow a few simple rules before, during and after cooking, we've nothing to worry about:

1 Keep raw and cooked foods separate.
2 If a bird is frozen, read the instructions carefully before you take off the wrapping. The bird must be thawed thoroughly and evenly, preferably in a fridge. The chicken's only ready for cooking when there are no ice crystals left in the cavity and you can move the leg joints freely.
3 Birds infected with salmonella can contaminate anything with which they come into contact. After use, knives and chopping boards should be washed or scrubbed, if necessary using a sanitiser, and make sure drips from the thawed-out chicken don't land on other food.
4 The chicken must be cooked right through. The Institute of Food Research says that it's best to do it without the stuffing in place, for the most even heat penetration. When you test it with a skewer, a cooked bird will ooze clear juice; if the liquid is bloody, it needs longer.
5 If keeping cooked chicken, cool as quickly as possible and store in the fridge, well away from anything uncooked.

Sales of fresh chicken have risen by more than one-third over the past five years. 45% of all the chicken we now buy is fresh, compared with 55% frozen. We asked Home Economics degree students from the Bath College of Higher Education to test fresh v frozen for us, together with Free-range, Corn-fed and Ready-basted birds, all roasted. They assessed them under three main headings: texture, flavour and value for money, and their preferences were as follows:

Texture
1 Fresh broiler
2 Free-range (the students found this 'chewy')
3 Frozen and Ready-basted (equal third)
4 Corn-fed

Flavour
1 Corn-fed (described as very 'gamey')
2 Free-range and fresh broiler equal second (the latter – unlike frozen chicken – is allowed to hang, which improves the flavour)
3 Ready-basted
4 Frozen

Value for money
1 Free-range
2 Frozen
3 Corn-fed
4 Fresh broiler
5 Ready-basted

On a points basis then, free-range was the overall winner, with fresh broiler second, corn-fed third and frozen fourth, just relegating ready-basted to last place.

It's a good idea to shop around and see what type of chicken you prefer. To help you enjoy the experiment, Michael has some excellent recipes for you to try.

CHICKEN AND LETTUCE PARCELS
Serves 4

Before we get into the cooking, a word about steaming, a technique required for this recipe. Steaming is not widely practised in Britain – at least not in comparison to baking, boiling, frying and grilling, but the equipment needed is nevertheless easily obtainable. A *Food and Drink* survey of steamers revealed that the cheapest (£5-6, made specially to fit standard saucepans) was the best value. Steaming is particularly good for vegetables, and, of course, chicken.

One of the problems with steamed foods is that they tend to be a little bland and unexciting. This technique takes care of that problem, using lettuce as a kind of edible cling film around chicken breasts that have been marinated for 2 hours in spices. It's a combination of French and Chinese techniques and goes well with delicately steamed vegetables, particularly courgettes.

4 breasts of chicken, skinned and boned
1 cos lettuce
8 oz (225g) rice
For the marinade sauce:
2 tbspns soy sauce
1 tbspn hoi sin sauce (from supermarkets
    or oriental grocers)
1 tspn fresh ginger, grated
½ cup water
1 tspn cornflour

Cut each chicken breast into two equal portions. Marinate the pieces in the soy sauce, hoi sin and ginger for 2 hours. Afterwards blanche the lettuce leaves in boiling salted water for 15-20 *seconds* only, drain and then wrap a lettuce leaf around each piece of chicken and place on a small plate. Place the plate in the steamer and steam vigorously for 12 minutes (you can cook the rice in the boiling water at the same time). Drain and make a bed of rice on a dish. Place the chicken parcels in a row on top of the rice. Pour the marinade into a saucepan and add the water and cornflour. Bring to the boil, stirring, and spoon over the chicken parcels.

ORIENTAL CHICKEN
Serves 4

This was the winning recipe for a main course from a *Food and Drink* competition. Participants had to devise a meal which could be cooked in 30 minutes, on a tight budget, and which would serve four people.

This dish by the Women's Institute team from Cumbria made outstanding use of fresh ingredients and contrasting soft and crunchy textures. It reflects the growing influence of eastern flavours in our food, and is extremely tasty served with brown rice (see below).

6 oz (175g) chicken meat, raw
1½ lbs (700g) carrots
2 oz (50g) margarine
5 fl oz (150ml) water
4 tbspns malt vinegar
3 tbspns soy sauce
2 level tbspns brown sugar
1 level tbspn cornflour
6 oz (175g) leeks, shredded
1 small fresh pineapple, peeled and chopped
5 oz (150g) beansprouts
2 oz (50g) flaked, toasted almonds

Discard skin from chicken and cut flesh into narrow strips. Cut carrots into 2-inch (5cm) pieces and then halve. Melt margarine in a frying-pan, add the chicken and carrots and sauté for 2-3 minutes, stirring. Cover and cook gently (shaking the pan occasionally to prevent sticking) for 15-20 minutes until carrots are tender. Stir water, vinegar, soy sauce and sugar into the pan. Blend cornflour with about 2 tablespoons of additional water into a smooth paste. Stir into pan. Add leeks and simmer for 3-4 minutes, stirring occasionally. Just before serving, stir in pineapple, beansprouts and almonds.

BROWN RICE
Serves 4

8 oz brown rice

Put rice in a saucepan, cover with cold, salted water and bring to the boil. Simmer for about 40 minutes or until just tender. Drain and serve.

NORMANDY STYLE CHICKEN
Serves 4

In Normandy in northern France there is a valley called the Auge, famous for its apples and its cream. This recipe is a product of the Auge's cooking combination.

I've adapted it to include fresh apple juice: a recent tasting revealed how superior in flavour this sort of juice is compared to that made from concentrates. You can easily sort out which is which in the shops – the concentrates have to declare it on the packet. With the fresh juices you can actually taste different apple varieties; altogether a better product. This recipe is a wonderful mixture of richness, sharpness and sweetness.

1 tbspn oil
1 chicken, cut into 4 joints
½ Spanish onion, chopped
Salt and freshly ground black pepper
10 fl oz (275ml) apple juice (fresh)
1 tbspn butter
2 Cox's apples, cored but not peeled
1 tspn cornflour
5 oz (150ml) double cream
A little chopped parsley

Heat the oil in a frying-pan and add the chicken joints and onion. Cook for 10 minutes until the chicken pieces are browned on both sides and the onions are translucent. Add seasoning. Pour enough apple juice to come almost halfway up the chicken and either simmer for 25 minutes or place in the oven at 350°F (180°C), gas mark 4 for 25 minutes.

Meanwhile, gently heat 1 tablespoon of butter in another pan. Cut the apples into 12 segments and fry for 3-4 minutes until golden brown. Keep warm.

Add the teaspoon of cornflour to the carton of cream and stir together. Blend it into the juices in the chicken pan and heat gently until it has thickened.

Place the fried apples on a serving dish and the chicken pieces next to them. Pour the sauce over the chicken and sprinkle with parsley just before serving.

CHICKEN STOCK

This wonderful broth (excellent on its own) is also the basis of many other dishes. Can you compare it to a stock cube? Don't bother: there is no comparison. To make really great chicken stock, however, you have to start with a chicken – or at least quite a lot of it. Certainly the giblets, but not the liver, it'll make the stock cloudy. The carcass is the real essential and (if you ever see them) things like wing tips or even carefully washed feet.

Put them in a pan with:
½ onion, stuck with 4 cloves
2 pints (1.1 litres) water
For the bouquet garni:
2 bay leaves
Stalks of a bunch of parsley
The central stem of a bunch of celery
2 sprigs of thyme

Simmer all the ingredients in the water for 45 minutes. Strain, remove the meat if you want to use it and keep the stock. Don't boil it and don't cook it longer – all you get is more 'bone' taste.

To remove the fat, chill the stock: the fat will float to the surface in a layer and is easy to spoon off. You can use the stock in soups, casseroles or with a few noodles or mushroom slices (plus seasoning) on its own.

CHICKEN II

THE ELASTIC CHICKEN

Three dishes for four people from one standard 3½ lb (1.6kg) chicken! If that seems to be stretching it a little, it's the reason for the name 'elastic chicken'.

First I'll explain how to cut up or 'joint' the bird: then I have two sets of crafty recipes. Each will give you the three dishes I have promised. In fact, this technique produces nine portions as well as the giblets and carcass. It's from this that the multiple meals come.

Before beginning the step-by-step cutting (illustrated overleaf), do make sure your chopping-board or work surface is large enough to give you plenty of room, and do use a really sharp knife. It should be between 5-8 inches (12.5-20.5 cm) long and have a good handle to give a safe grip. If you know how to sharpen it on a steel, do so, before you begin.

● Cut all the trussing string off. Move the legs and wings to loosen them and remove giblets from inside the bird.
● Pull the legs away from the sides and, cutting from the neck end as close to the body as possible, sever the skin between body and leg. Then separate the joint with the knife and the leg will come away from the body. Repeat on the other side.
● Put legs skin side down and separate drumstick and thigh by cutting firmly down the line of fat over the joint. If you follow the line carefully, you'll be amazed at how easy this is.
● Draw around the base of each wing with the knife, cutting to the bone. Twist the wing and separate the joint with the knife.
● Cut down the fat line on the sides of the chicken breast starting at the tail end, separating the breast from the back.
● Lay the breast flat and cut off a third at the pointed end.
● Turn the breast over, split lengthways and you're ready!

(Practice helps. After two or three goes, you'll find it easy to cut along the fat lines and you'll be able to separate the joints with little effort.)

Here are two ways of using the pieces from the elastic chicken: the first set consists of a French dish, a soup and some pancakes; the second set is an Italian dish, a Scottish soup and a Chinese stir-fry. Whichever you use, you'll feed four people very well three times over, from just one ordinary chicken.

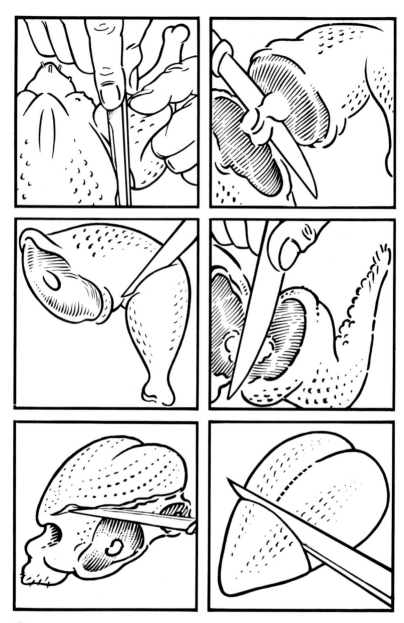

CUTTING UP A CHICKEN

THE FIRST SET

1 CHICKEN PROVENÇAL
Serves 4-6

A rich and sunny chicken casserole that can be cooked on top of the stove as well as in the oven. Olives, anchovies, tomatoes and herbs combine to make the famous French provençal flavour. It's often served with wide, flat noodles to take up the sauce, although rice is nice with it too. If you can't find any passata, liquidised or sieved tinned tomatoes are an alternative.

2 tbspns olive oil
6 joints chicken (2 breasts, 2 thighs, 2 drumsticks)
1 onion, chopped
1 red pepper, chopped
1 clove garlic, crushed
½ × 1¾-pint (1 litre) jar passata (see page 13)
1 tspn dried basil and oregano (mixed)
Salt and freshly ground black pepper
4 anchovy fillets
6 black olives

Heat the oil in a deep frying-pan and fry the chicken pieces until brown on both sides. Add the onion, pepper, garlic, passata and herbs and season to taste. Stir and cook for about 25 minutes until the chicken is tender and cooked through. Serve garnished with the anchovy fillets and olives.

2 CHICKEN AND SWEETCORN SOUP
Serves 4-6

A simple Chinese-style soup that is a particular favourite with children. Use the wings to make a good stock for this (turn back to page 39 for method). It makes a great start to an exotic meal or a good basis for a family supper with some pancake rolls or hot French bread and cheese to follow.

2 pints (1.1 litre) of chicken stock
1 × 1lb (450g) can creamed sweetcorn
1 dspn cornflour
1 tbspn soy sauce
2 tbspns chicken meat (from wings), chopped
Salt and freshly ground black pepper
2 spring onions, finely chopped

Skim surface fat from cooled stock and discard. Mix together the sweetcorn and cornflour and empty into a food processor or liquidiser with the stock and soy sauce. Liquidise for up to 1 minute, depending on preferred consistency. (If you haven't got a blender, pass the mixture through a sieve.)

Add chicken and seasoning and heat through, stirring. Serve sprinkled with the spring onions.

3 DIJON CHICKEN PANCAKES
Serves 4

You can make your own pancakes for this or buy the ready-made French ones available in packs of 10 in most supermarkets. They are a real convenience food!

Cooked chicken from the breast joint
8 oz (225g) button mushrooms, sliced
1 tspn Dijon mustard
Salt and freshly ground black pepper
8 pancakes
2 oz (50g) Gruyère or Cheddar cheese, grated
For the white sauce:
10 fl oz (275ml) milk
1 tspn butter
1 tspn flour

Make the white sauce by whisking sauce ingredients together until thick, over a medium heat. (This is a crafty method of making a basic béchamel sauce which I find a great time-saver.) Add the chicken, mushrooms, mustard and seasoning to the white sauce. Divide mixture between the pancakes, piling it into the centre of each. Fold over two opposite sides to meet in the middle. Then fold in remaining sides to make a neat parcel. Arrange in an ovenproof dish (fold side down) and sprinkle with the cheese. Heat through in oven at 350°F (180°C), gas mark 4 for about 20 minutes..

Jill's wine recommendations:
It is merely a matter of personal preference whether you go for red or white wine to go with chicken. Among reds, the light and medium styles are best, particularly those with unusually pronounced bouquets, such as Beaujolais and Rioja. White wines with body and depth are a good choice, and the Chardonnay grape makes just such a wine wherever it is grown in the world.

THE SECOND SET

1 CHICKEN FLORENTINE
Serves 4

This classic combination of spinach and cheese comes from Florence and traditionally accompanies fish or eggs, but I find it particularly good with chicken.

You can use frozen leaf spinach if you must, but there is no comparison with fresh leaves blanched in boiling water for 30 seconds before use.

2 chicken breasts and 2 thighs
10 fl oz (275ml) water
1 bayleaf
1 onion
1 lb (450g) leaf spinach
1 tspn butter, melted
4 oz (110g) grated cheese (Gruyère or Cheddar)
½ tspn nutmeg, grated
10 fl oz (275 ml) white sauce (for method see page 45)

Poach the chicken pieces for 20 minutes in the water with the bayleaf and onion. Cool and then bone them, leaving the flesh in large pieces. Toss the blanched spinach in the butter and line a fireproof dish with it. Lay the chicken on top in a layer. Mix the nutmeg and 3 ounces (75g) of the cheese into the white sauce. Pour the sauce over the chicken, sprinkle with the rest of the cheese and bake for 15 minutes at 375°F (190°C), gas mark 5, until the cheese sauce bubbles.

2 COCKIE LEEKIE SOUP
Serves 4

A Scottish soup of heartening flavour and some unusual ingredients. Have courage: the prunes are traditional and the tastes do go wonderfully together. Serve with hot oat bread.

Chicken carcass and wings
1 lb (450g) leeks, cut in 2-inch (5cm) lengths
8 oz (225g) prunes
Salt and freshly ground black pepper

Poach the carcass and wings in water for an hour. Strain, pick the meat from the bones and return to the stock. Add the leeks, prunes and seasoning. Simmer for 30 minutes until the leeks are tender.

3 CHINESE CHICKEN AND PEPPERS
Serves 4

This is a stir-fry dish that would traditionally be made in a wok. Do use it if you've got one, if not a deep frying-pan does almost as well. Do get it thoroughly hot at the beginning — the secret of stir-frying is fast cooking, to seal the food and steam it in its own juices. Should be served immediately on a bed of rice.

1 red pepper
1 green pepper
1 Spanish onion
Chicken meat from the drumsticks
    and separated breast joint (uncooked)
1 tbspn oil
For the sauce:
2 tspns each Soy sauce and water
1 tspn each brown sugar, cornflour, lemon juice

Slice the peppers and onions in ¼-inch (0.5cm) strips.
    Cut the chicken meat into small pieces and fry for 2 minutes in the oil in the hot pan.
    Take the chicken out and set aside. Fry the peppers and onions for 2 minutes over a high heat, and return the chicken to the pan.
    Mix the sauce ingredients till smooth and add to the pan, stirring until the sauce thickens and turns shiny.

Meat

When Lord Sieff, Honorary President of Marks & Spencer, told a group of farmers recently that roast pork and grilled pork had lost their flavour, he revived a debate which always arouses strong feelings.

In terms of technological innovation, the raising of pigs has been one of the success stories of the past decade. Advances in breeding, feeding and environment have helped pork maintain, and even improve, its place in the meat market. While high street sales of beef and lamb have been declining, pork sales have actually increased slightly over the past two years. Part of the reason is price. Producers have been able to keep pork prices down by breeding animals with less fat on them; the leaner the pig, the smaller the amount of food it needs to grow.

Which brings us back to Lord Sieff. There are those who argue that it's this very absence of fat which has caused the lack of flavour he was complaining about. It's a point of view we even heard from a Hull pig farmer who confirmed that his porkers are bred leaner for the supermarkets, but who said that he personally preferred fattier cuts.

Is that the way most of us feel? Well, according to the Institute of Food Research at Bristol, the answer is 'yes' – but only just. Together with the Meat and Livestock Commission, the Institute carried out the most comprehensive study ever of the eating quality of British pork. For a start, they discovered that flavour doesn't come particularly high on our list of requirements; it ranks lower than leanness, tenderness and juiciness. In carefully controlled tests, Dr Jeff Wood and his colleagues compared the reactions of their subjects to pork with a third of an inch (8mm) of fat on it, and pork with a fat covering of two-thirds of an inch (16mm). By narrow percentage margins, the fattier pork was found to be juicier and more tender than the leaner variety; when it came to flavour, however, the control group expressed no preference. Sceptics might be tempted to conclude that most of us have forgotten (or have never known) how pork used to taste before it was farmed intensively to satisfy today's enormous demands. However, the important thing is that if you want to buy meat raised in the traditional way (without added hormones, tenderisers or growth promoters) you can still find it – if you know where to look.

Anne Petch, who farms at King's Nympton in Devon, puts flavour first. During the 1970s she began to take an interest in the Gloucester Old Spot, a breed then so rare that there were probably only 200 breeding sows in the country. (How quickly things change: up until the 1930s it was one of our chief breeds.) Gradually she built up a herd, incorporating other old breeds, like Tamworths, Middle Whites, Berkshires and, more recently, Large Blacks.

Unlike factory-reared pigs, which are taken from their mothers at 10 days old or less and then put in tiered racks like battery chickens, Anne's are allowed to develop naturally. Fed on 'honest-to-goodness' barley and wheat from the local mill, they produce meat which 'stands well to the knife', and has lovely crisp crackling.

When Anne first took her pigs to the abattoir she was told that they didn't conform to modern specifications; the grading system was purely mathematical and took no account of eating qualities. Undaunted, and encouraged by the enthusiasm of her friends (who knew a good thing when they ate it), she said to herself, 'It doesn't have to be like this. Let's go for the best we can and charge accordingly.' In going for the best, she has welcomed the advice of the experts at the Institute of Food Research. Anne Petch's farm butchery now offers an impressive choice, including basic joints (with speciality butchering for restaurants); smoked hams (Lord Sieff must approve of these because Marks & Spencer use them in their staff training); smoked raw pork tenderloin; smoked bacon and eight varieties of sausage. Anne also sells pedigree Devon beef, produced on neighbouring farms, which is allowed to hang for three weeks. 'You could cut it with a butter knife' she says proudly.

If you'd like to judge for yourself how her meat compares with what's available in supermarkets, the address to write to is:

Anne Petch
Heal Farm Quality Traditional Meats
King's Nympton
Umberleigh
Devon EX37 9TB

Heal Farm can supply price lists, the story of the product, and information about rare breeds of pig. Please enclose a stamped addressed envelope.

Further east, in Sussex, Ray Gould farms to exactly the same traditional standards. He specialises in magnificent beef (the offspring of Charollais bulls and Hereford X Friesian cows) raised without so much as a whiff of artificial aid. 'The only reason for using steroids and growth promoters', he says, 'is to produce good beef out of bad cattle.'

'Factory' bull calves, their growth prematurely promoted, are ready for slaughter at 14 months. Injected with tenderisers before they're despatched, they can be sold less than a week later. Ray Gould's cattle, by contrast, are slaughtered at 1½-2 years, without benefit of additives, and hung to mature for up to three weeks. In consequence, his beef is darker in colour and full of flavour.

Like Anne Petch, Ray has developed an appetising range for sale to the public, including half a dozen types of sausage, and butter and ice-cream made from untreated milk. For more information, send a stamped addressed envelope to:

Ray Gould
Old Spot Farm
Piltdown
Nr Uckfield
E. Sussex

There are many other 'organic' meat producers in the country. For more information, write to: British Organic Farmers/Soil Association, 86 Colston St, Bristol BS1 5BB
The current edition of the British Country Foods trade directory is also helpful. For more on that, send a stamped addressed envelope to:

Eve Thomson
4, St Mary's Place
Stamford
Lincolnshire PE9 2DN

Anton Mosimann's Poached Fillet of Beef
Serves 4

This recipe represents the ultimate development of cuisine naturelle: Anton's healthy diet for gourmets.

It uses steak, but in a technique he has only recently perfected. Like many top chefs' recipes, it may seem a little brief. When he mentions 'garnishing the steak with vegetables of choice', I suggest you make thin matchstick (or 'julienne') strips of carrot and leeks or celeriac and spring onions. Poach these in the stock for 3 minutes before using them, both as a decoration and vegetable accompaniment, instead of (or as well as) the raw chopped vegetables.

4 × 5 oz (150g) fillet steaks, well trimmed of fat
15 fl oz (400 ml) brown veal stock, well flavoured with garlic (if desired)
Salt and freshly ground black pepper

Garnish the steaks with vegetables of choice.

Heat the stock until it is simmering and then poach the beef fillets for 4 minutes.

Serve the beef on a plate surrounded with freshly chopped raw vegetables such as carrots, celeriac and peppers.

Jill's wine recommendations:
The red clarets of Bordeaux are a classic accompaniment to hearty beef dishes and casseroles, and a similar style of wine can be expected from Cabernet Sauvignon wines from around the world. The cheapest usually come from Eastern European countries and South America. Nearer home, the Dãos of Portugal have the guts to match most red meat dishes.

POT-ROASTED SILVERSIDE

Serves 4-6

It's a cliché of cuisine that slow cooking brings out the flavour and that the tougher, cheaper cuts are better tasting than many more expensive ones. Like many clichés, however, it happens to be true. There are ways of cooking the middle range of joints (like silverside) that our time-pressed age seems to forget. Pot-roasting is one of these ways and it's a technique that's worth reviving. Not only does it create delicious, moist joints of meat, it also cooks with the minimum of fat and makes its own sauce.

Although I suggest silverside for this dish, you can use a number of 'braising' joints, like Aitch bone or short ribs, with equal success. All produce a slightly spicy, herb-flavoured alternative to the traditional roast beef.

1 × 3lb (1.4 kg) silverside
2 onions
4 cloves
1 lb (450g) carrots
4 tbspns cider (*not* malt) vinegar
1 bay leaf
2 parsley stalks
1 celery leaf
½ cup water

Heat an ovenproof pan until very hot, on the top of the stove. Cook the joint on all sides for 2-3 minutes until 'sealed'. This will cause some spluttering, but don't worry: just open a window!

Take the joint out. Cut the onions in half, stick each half with a clove and put in the pan. Tie the bay leaf, parsley stalks and celery leaf together and put into the pan with the carrot. Splash in the vinegar, let it sizzle, add the water and put the meat on top.

Cover and cook in the oven at 300°F (150°C), gas mark 2 for 2½ hours. Remove the meat and leave to stand for 5 minutes before carving. Discard herbs and cloves. Serve the carrots with the meat and purée the onions with the juices for a sauce.

MYRTLE ALLEN'S IRISH STEW
Serves 4

On one of his many trips across the sea to Ireland in the cause of culinary science, Chris Kelly managed to 'land on his feet' at the restaurant of one of the most famous chefs in the land, that of Myrtle Allen. She not only runs a successful restaurant in her own country but has an equally popular one in Paris (where else?) selling Irish special- ities. Quite an achievement!

Her success and, indeed, her cooking, deserves respect. This is her recipe for Irish Stew. Like many dishes that were originally just rural traditions, Irish Stew in its pure form has been much argued over. In particular, you'll notice that she doesn't cube the lamb, which some self-appointed purists would take issue with. I wouldn't argue any more; just cook the recipe, not forgetting to skim the fat from the stock before serving: it makes all the difference.

8 lamb chops or pieces (best end, middle neck or stewing lamb)
3 carrots, cut into large chunks
2 onions, quartered
4 potatoes
1 pint (570ml) of warmed stock (preferably lamb)
Parsley for garnishing
Salt and freshly ground black pepper

Cut spare fat off the lamb and put fat in a pan to be rendered down to liquid. Fry the meat lightly in the fat to seal, and put to one side. Do the same with the carrots and onions and put a layer of them in the bottom of a casserole with a little seasoning. Place the meat on top and cover with the remaining carrots and onions. Put the whole potatoes on top and pour the warmed stock over.

Cook for 1½ hours in a moderate oven at 350°F (180°C), gas mark 4. (In March, when the lamb is very young, cooking may only take 30-40 minutes.)

Skim the fat off the top and serve in deep bowls.

SAUSAGES

When we were doing a *Food and Drink* sausage testing and tasting, we needed so many sausages cooked we had to call in someone used to doing them in large quantities. That somebody was an army chef at Aldershot and his method was a great revelation to me. No pan, no grill, no pricking or prodding. He used a hot oven (400°F, 200°C, or gas mark 6) and racks laid over baking trays full of hot water.

The sausages went straight onto the racks and into the oven. The heat cooked the skins crisp while the steam from the water plumped up the bangers and stopped the fat splashing. All in all, a great way to fry (if, indeed, frying it is)! You may only find it worth using if you are cooking a lot of sausages or if the oven's already hot, but it certainly is an excellent method – and surprisingly similar to the crafty way to cook turkey (see page 102).

If you fancy doing something a little more adventurous than just plain sausages, why not try Hereford sausages? Why this recipe should have developed in Hereford I'm not sure; maybe it was designed for beef sausages made from Hereford cattle. I certainly prefer beef sausages for this country recipe, which manages to turn sausages and onions into a square meal.

HEREFORD SAUSAGES
Serves 4

You can cook this in the oven with a covering of quarter-inch (0.5 cm) slices of potato, for a dish of scalloped Hereford sausages, or serve it as it is with 'mash'.

1 lb (450g) sausages
1 lb (450g) onions, sliced
8 oz (225g) eating apples, peeled, cored and sliced
Salt and freshly ground black pepper
10 fl oz (275ml) apple juice (preferably fresh)
1 tspn thyme and marjoram, mixed

Gently fry the sausages in their own fat for 5 minutes. Remove from the pan and set aside. Fry the onions and apples gently for 5 minutes more. Put the sausages back in, add seasoning, apple juice and herbs and simmer for 40 minutes.

TWO HOME-MADE SAUSAGE RECIPES

Neither of these recipes use skins – which makes them much easier to do at home – and both are delicious in the role of more conventional bangers at breakfast or high tea.

In the first, the meat recipe comes from the tradition of sausage-making in the US. A mixture that in Europe would be cased in skin, is shaped into a pattie by hand and then fried. I don't know why bangers changed when they crossed the Atlantic – maybe the Americans couldn't be bothered to coax the mixture into skins. Quite right – I can't either. The recipe needs a food processor or mincer.

HERBED SAUSAGE PATTIES
Serves 4

12 oz (350g) lean beef
4 oz (110g) beef kidney suet
4 oz (110g) soft breadcrumbs
1 egg
1 tspn each marjoram, sage and thyme
Salt and freshly ground black pepper
Flour to coat
A little oil

Mince or process the beef until it's a smooth purée (the butcher will do this for you if asked). Then mince or process the suet into small dice and add to the beef. Stir in the breadcrumbs, egg, herbs and seasoning. Knead well for 2 minutes. Rest for 5 minutes. Divide into eight, mould into hamburger shapes, coat with flour and fry for 5 minutes a side in very little oil. Serve hot or cold.

Jill's wine recommendations:
Sausages are, to a banger, rather fatty, and therefore need a light, 'rapier-like' white or red wine to cut through to the flavour. Surprisingly, a better choice than a heavy red. And, incidentally, white wine is good for cooking sausages in, too, making a delicious tart sauce. Good examples to go for are the 'new-style' slim-line white Riojas, any red Gamay wines and all red Nouveaux.

GLAMORGAN SAUSAGES
Serves 4

It may come as some surprise to find, in a chapter entitled 'meat', a recipe which uses no meat at all. These are really cheese rissoles, originally made with the now defunct Glamorgan cheese. Savoury, delicious and as appealing to meat-eaters as vegetarians.

I make these sausages out of Cheddar or Lancashire cheese. Cheese that has gone hard is fine but blue cheese won't do. You must use either fresh breadcrumbs or bread soaked in milk: the golden crumbs out of a packet are not right for this (or most other recipes).

8 oz (225g) breadcrumbs
4 fl oz (100ml) milk
8 oz (225g) strong-flavoured cheese
1 tspn English mustard
3 tbspns mixed fresh herbs: parsley, thyme and either chives or
    spring onion, chopped
3 eggs, separated

Soak 6 oz (175g) of the breadcrumbs in the milk, reserving 2 oz (50g) for later. Mix the cheese, milk-soaked breadcrumbs, mustard, herbs and the egg yolks together. Knead well and divide into eight. Roll into sausage shapes and firm with your hands.

Beat the egg whites, roll the sausages first in them and then in the remaining 2 oz (50g) of crumbs. Leave to set for 10 minutes. Fry for 10-12 minutes over a low heat as for conventional sausages and watch they don't 'catch'.

Exotic vegetables

Mooli, okra, Chinese leaves, sweet potatoes; initially they were known in the wholesale trade as 'queer gear', but now 'exotic' vegetables are becoming so widely available in the UK that pretty soon we'll be dropping the 'exotic' altogether and taking them as much for granted as peas and cabbage.

The immigrant communities throughout the UK are to be thanked for these tasty alternatives, which ought to benefit British cuisine enormously. But many cooks are being characteristically cautious about experimenting, reasoning with true Anglo-Saxon phlegm, 'better the carrots you know than the plantains you don't'. Incidentally, in case you haven't come across plantains, they're the ones that look like fat bananas but can't be enjoyed raw. Michael's tips on how to cook them can be found towards the end of this chapter.

Of course, all vegetables were exotic once, even potatoes. When a Spanish monk first brought them back home from the Andes in the second half of the sixteenth century, they were viewed with great suspicion. People used to planting seeds thought these bulbous tubers looked as though they might well be the devil's work. Introduced to Ireland and mainland Britain by adventurers like Drake and Raleigh, the potato was equally slow to catch on here. It remained a curiosity, only to be glimpsed in the gardens of aristocrats. For their part, the Scots would have no truck at all with the indelicate-looking upstart, because it wasn't mentioned in the Bible.

With the drift to the towns, triggered by the Industrial Revolution, the nineteenth century saw the beginning of the potato's golden age: it was cheap food for the masses. At the same time, the catastrophic and repeated failure of the crop led to the development of blight-resistant varieties.

By the turn of the twentieth century, potatoes were very big business indeed and speculators in the market grew rich. Those determined enough would pay anything up to £50 for a single tuber. A Scottish farmer, one Archie Finlay, was offered £20,000 for his stock of sought-after Eldorado tubers. (He turned it down.) The present-day chairman of the National Vegetable Society, Donald MacLean, has been campaigning on behalf of the potato for many years, and he brought its history up to date for me. Incredibly, there are now more than 100 varieties grown in Britain, 'But how many do you find in supermarkets? Six if you're lucky. Where are the rest hiding?'

If you're interested in trying some of the more unusual varieties, such as Edgecote Purple; the blue Arran Victory; or May Queen, which is ready in spring, you will have to grow them yourself. For a guide to the problems and possibilities, including advice on which types can be raised in containers, you couldn't do better than contact Donald Mac-Lean himself. Donald knows, and genuinely loves, everything about potatoes. 'The vehicle to a better quality life', he calls them (making them sound a bit like a sports car) but he means it. You can write to him, enclosing a stamped addressed envelope, at:

Dornock Farm
Crieff
Perthshire, PH7 3QN

The tomato is a member of the potato family, too, and its story has many parallels. Originating, like its cousin, in Latin America, the tomato was also brought to Europe in the late sixteenth century. It was originally prized simply for its flowers; the fruit was thought to be poisonous. When we learned better, we called it the love-apple for a while. As the tomato reached its current peak of popularity, we started to make the same mistakes as we did with the potato. Variety and subtlety have been sacrificed on the altar of convenience and profit. We demand home-grown tomatoes all the year round and supermarkets duly provide them. But where has all the flavour gone? The fruit looks perfectly round and healthily red but it often doesn't taste of anything much. Varieties like the ubiquitous Moneymaker, favoured by growers for its high yield and reliable uniformity, tend to be as bland as tap-water. It's tempting to lay some of the blame on early picking (while the fruit's still green), which ensures longer shelf life. The main reason, however, is that growers are forced by the supermarkets to provide uniformly shaped, tough-skinned tomatoes. And they have to provide 'high-cropping' varieties because otherwise they'd go out of business. The same applies, incidentally, to growers in Europe, particularly the Dutch, who now dominate the market. Faced with the problem of the tasteless tomato, we went to the fount of all horticultural wisdom, *Gardeners' Question Time.* 'What's to be done?' we asked. 'Simple!' they replied, in unison; 'Grow your own.'

The varieties they particularly recommended are Gardener's Delight; the yellow-fruited Golden Sunrise; and Tigerella. Not to be outdone, dozens of viewers (who wholeheartedly sympathised with our lament) sent us their own suggestions. Here are a couple of them, so that the amateurs are represented alongside the professionals. Mr Hale of Brixham swears by Piranto (he kindly enclosed two seeds) and

Seamus O'Reilly from Dublin has high praise for Ailsa Craig Leader, which, he says, isn't a prodigious cropper but has a lovely taste.

One glimmer of hope on the horizon is that a few growers are now experimenting with smaller, 'cherry' tomatoes (mostly the Gardeners' Delight variety). These are sweeter and better-flavoured. Marks & Spencer's, for one, are stocking them when they're in season. Let's hope that they prove a success.

GREEK TOMATO SALAD
Serves 4

One of my favourite hot-weather dishes is this eastern Mediterranean-style tomato salad.

Given a really warm day, whether in Crete or Cleethorpes, these flavours and textures seem absolutely made for each other. I've eaten it for lunch at a beachside villa every day for a week and not tired of the taste. On cold winter days, if you can find the essential ingredient – sweet tasty tomatoes – it can bring back memories of summer warmth and relaxation.

You can just eat it on its own with hot French or sesame seed bread, but it also goes well with grills and kebabs. Don't use any cheese other than the Greek fetta – a white, salty and very crumbly sheep's milk cheese, widely available – if you can't find it, leave out the cheese.

1 lb (450g) cherry tomatoes
½ Spanish onion, thinly sliced
2 oz (50g) fetta cheese
3-4 black olives
For the dressing:
⅓ cup lemon juice
⅔ cup olive oil
1 tspn sugar
½ tspn salt
1 tspn basil (preferably fresh, finely chopped)

Wash the tomatoes and cut them into quarters. Place them in a bowl and add the onion. Crumble the Fetta cheese over the tomatoes and onion and lastly add the olives.

To prepare the dressing, mix the lemon juice, olive oil, sugar and salt together. When blended, pour over the salad and leave to stand for a few minutes before serving.

GRILLED TOMATOES PROVENÇAL

Grilled tomatoes in the South of France are a course on their own, often at a lunchtime meal. They must, however, be the giant Marmande or beef tomatoes, weighing up to a pound (450g) each; they must be generously seasoned and grilled until the top is black and the whole vegetable is hot and juicy.

Per person:
1 beef tomato
1 clove garlic, crushed
½ tspn salt
1 tspn fresh parsley, finely chopped
1 tspn breadcrumbs
1 tspn olive oil

Cut the tomato in half across its equator. Place both halves (skin side down) in a shallow earthenware grilling dish. Score the cut side of the tomato halves with a sharp knife in a criss-cross pattern, to allow the flavour to penetrate while cooking.

Mix the crushed garlic and salt together and spread equal amounts on each half of the tomato. Then put the finely chopped parsley and breadcrumbs over the top. Lastly, pour half a teaspoon of oil over each half. Press down to make the topping firm.

Grill for 10 minutes until the top is blackened. Eat quickly while hot!

ARTICHOKES

Of all the 'exotic' vegetables we can now find on the supermarket shelves, the artichoke least deserves the name. It has been part of our diet since Elizabethan times and recipes for it abound in nineteenth century cookery books. Perhaps it is the spiky leaves and the 'choke' at the centre that have put people off. This recipe does away with both problems before the vegetable reaches the plate.

Buy young artichokes, not too mauve and with pliable leaves. Trim the stem off level and turn the leaves down with scissors to the height of the closed heart.

Per person:
1 pint (570ml) water
Juice of half a lemon
1 tspn salt
1 artichoke
4 tbspns mayonnaise (or Hollandaise Sauce)

Bring the water to the boil, add the lemon juice, salt and artichokes, cooking at a steady boil for 20 minutes. Take the artichokes out and drain upside down. Holding each artichoke in a folded tea towel and using a strong tablespoon, scoop out all the leaves near the top that are closed off into a bud. Underneath there is the hairy choke; scrape that off carefully (underneath it is the heart, the best part).

If eating hot, place on individual plates and fill the cup in the centre with Hollandaise sauce. If you want to eat them cold, let them cool in the fridge and fill with mayonnaise. Either way, to eat them you need to pull off each leaf, dip in the sauce and eat the soft end, discarding the 'woody' parts. When all the leaves are gone, eat the heart.

EXOTIC STIR-FRY
Serves 4

This Chinese-style dish teams up two newcomers with an established exotic vegetable, the red pepper – a sweet relative of the fiery chilli. The first of the newcomers is snow peas, similar to mange tout, they're a delicate pea that never develops much 'pea' but the pods of which are delicious.

They can be cooked in boiling water for 5 minutes and eaten like peas, or stir-fried as here. The other ingredient is mooli, which looks like a white carrot, but is actually a giant radish. You can use it grated in salads, or as a hot vegetable, very low in calories but good on flavour.

The colours of this stir-fry are so bright and attractive it's worth serving on its own as a separate course. It's very simple but quite exciting, both to cook and eat.

1 tbspn cooking oil
1 tspn fresh ginger, finely chopped
1 clove garlic, crushed
8 oz (225g) snow peas
8 oz (225g) mooli, peeled
1 red pepper
Pinch of salt
1 dspn soy sauce

Pour the oil into a hot, heavy-based frying-pan or wok (see page 26). When the oil has heated up, add the ginger and garlic and leave to fry for 1 minute.

Meanwhile, string the snow peas (as you would runner beans) and chop the mooli and red pepper into pieces the same size as the snow peas. (If all the same size, the vegetables take the same amount of time to cook.)

Put all the vegetables into the hot pan and stir, gently and continuously, for 1-1½ minutes. Add salt and the soy sauce. Continue stirring for another minute and then serve while the vegetables still have a crisp bite to them.

Purée of Celeriac

Serves 4-6

In France and Italy celeriac is often eaten raw, very much as we eat celery, but I prefer it cooked. Celeriac is large and knobbly, like an aggressive turnip, has a celery flavour and can turn one of our everyday dishes – mashed potatoes – into a gourmet treat. Serve with rich food such as pheasant casserole or rosemary-flavoured roast lamb. The almost nutty celeriac flavour comes through strongly but not over-whelmingly. Celeriac, by the way, is mostly available during the winter months.

1 lb (450g) celeriac
2 lb (900g) potatoes
5 fl oz (150ml) semi-skimmed milk, heated
12 tbspns fromage frais (see page 17) or butter
Salt and freshly ground back pepper

Peel the celeriac and potatoes and chop into 1-inch (2.5cm) cubes. Boil in salted water for 15 minutes. Mash thoroughly and add the heated milk and then the fromage frais. Whisk well until smooth and lightly season.

Jill's wine recommendations:

Where these vegetable dishes are being served as an accompaniment to the main dish, this should dictate the choice of wines. When the more garlicky recipes are being served as a course on their own, go for the cheapest drinkable red wine you can find ... it'll probably be fighting a losing battle anyway.

FRIED PLANTAIN
Serves 4

A truly tropical exotic vegetable, a plantain looks like a banana with big ideas. Don't be deceived by their appearance into trying to eat them raw though: they can draw your mouth like a lemon. They are eaten boiled, mashed or, best of all, fried.

In the West Indies, where they come from, frying is the favourite method, especially as a side dish to a fiery goat curry or chicken fricassee. They have a sweet but hearty taste that goes well with highly flavoured foods. You can season them with salt or soft brown sugar, according to your taste or the dish they accompany.

2 plantains
4 tbspns plain flour
1 tspn cinnamon (or allspice)
Oil to fry

Peel the plantains and cut them at an angle widthways into ½-inch (1cm) slices. Mix the flour and cinnamon and dip the slices to coat them.

Fry flat in ¼ inch (0.5cm) of hot oil until crisp on both sides, about 2 minutes per side. Drain off the oil and serve immediately – they go soggy if kept waiting.

POTATO TRIO

Here are three ways of making the most of this once exotic but now commonplace vegetable. First, how to make perfect roast potatoes: something much desired but rarely achieved. . . .

CRISPY ROAST POTATOES

King Edward or Desirée make delicious roast potatoes. Parsnips are also delicious when roasted by this method.

Peel and cut the potatoes into even-sized pieces. Parboil in salted water for 8 minutes. Meanwhile, heat some vegetable oil – 2 tablespoons of oil for every 2 pounds (900g) potatoes – in a roasting tin in the oven at 350°F (180°C), gas mark 4 until very hot. Drain the potatoes and place in roasting tin, turning them to coat with oil. Cook for 35-40 minutes until golden and crispy. (If you're using a fan oven, you may need to cook at a higher heat, with the potatoes in a covered dish.)

ANTON MOSIMANN'S POTATO DISH
Serves 4-6

Anton Mosimann of the Dorchester, in his now-famous excursion north of the Trent to cook lunch for a Sheffield family, provided a variation on the potato theme. For me, the greatest pleasure of the film wasn't just the food but watching his knife-work, the blade slipping through the potatoes in wafer-thin slices too quickly for the naked eye – much like a conjuring trick.

1½ lbs (700g) of peeled potatoes, thinly sliced
1 large onion, thinly sliced
Salt and freshly ground black pepper
Pinch of ground nutmeg
A little vegetable or chicken stock

Put the onion slices in an oven-proof dish and place in a hot oven for 2 minutes. Remove the dish and cover with the potato slices. Season, sprinkle with nutmeg and then moisten with a little stock. Cover and cook at 400°F (200°C), gas mark 6, for 40 minutes.

Pommes de Terre Dauphinoise
Serves 4

To finish the potato trio, a dish from France that's become a classic in that country of classic recipes, and is one of my absolute favourites. It's a way of cooking potatoes that makes them a dish to be savoured on their own. It's traditionally served with roast lamb or beef, or grilled veal kidneys.

Although it's rich, if served to four people, each gets only 2 table-spoons of cream and a dessertspoon of butter. Not *too* bad for some-thing that tastes as superbly self-indulgent as Pommes de Terre Dauphinoise.

Whether or not you're a vegetarian, turn into one for a day, just to try this as a main course perhaps with one or two other vegetables to set it off, or just salad and wholemeal bread.

1 clove garlic, cut in half
1 butter paper
1½ lbs (700g) King Edward potatoes, thinly sliced
Salt and freshly ground black pepper
2 oz (50g) butter
5 fl oz (150ml) double cream
5 fl oz (150ml) semi-skimmed milk

Rub the inside of an earthenware dish with the cut sides of the clove of garlic and leave to dry. Then grease the dish with the butter paper. Place a layer of potato slices in the dish. Add seasoning and spread a little of the butter over the top. Repeat this process until all the potatoes have been used up and are evenly layered. Then add the double cream and milk mixed together. Dot with remaining butter. Cook for 30 minutes at 400°F (200°C), gas mark 6 and then for another 30 minutes at 350°F (180°C), gas mark 4.

After 1 hour, the potatoes should be browned on the surface and golden and creamy on the inside.

PUDDINGS

There was a time when a cartoonist might have caricatured the two sides in any debate on healthy eating as Cranks and Fatties. Since it began to sink in, however, that the UK is near the top of the world heart-disease league, things seem to have changed dramatically. The relentless drumming home of the message about sensible diet has to some extent worked, so that there's now a third group in the middle of the cartoon, much larger than either of the other two, labelled Most Of Us. But along with an increasing awareness of the need to reform our eating and exercise habits has come an interesting and contradictory side-effect. When the Ted Bates advertising agency did a survey of consumer attitudes they found that, although we have actually received the message, we haven't fully understood it. Their research revealed that while sales of semi-skimmed milk are up, so are sales of chocolate and custard. What we're doing, according to the Bates agency, is obeying the healthy-eating rules some of the time and then rewarding ourselves for being good. The same goes for exercise. We may ride a bike to work and play squash once a week, but, in the warm after-glow of virtuousness we tend to give ourselves prizes of cream cakes or suet pudding. Naturally, the advertisers aren't slow to put temptation in our way either.

The Ted Bates agency have christened it all The Body Balance Theory, and balance is a word close to the heart of *Food and Drink*. We are concerned to promote and encourage the buying and cooking of things that are positively good for us all, but at the same time we're determined not to lose sight of the fact that food can mean pure enjoyment, too. I love puddings – both eating and making them – and I've no intention whatsoever of giving them up, even though I fully understand that scoffing profiteroles twice a day wouldn't exactly 'prolong active life'. The point is that, as part of a balanced, sensible, enjoyable diet, the occasional pudding has its place.

For a nation which invented the pudding (well, if we didn't, who did?) we haven't shown much imagination. To look at the everyday domestic menu, you'd think that we were still living in a pre-industrialised society. Now that the majority don't burn masses of calories with hard, physical labour, there's sense in looking at alternatives to Plum Duff and Spotted Dick; not that they aren't delicious as well.

Hans, a German genius who runs the Confiserie Schweitzer in Cambridge (for my money one of the best in Britain) says, very diplomatically, that what we need in the pudding department is 'a little revolution'. He'd like to see us being more daring in terms of variety, colour, lightness and subtlety, not just in the cooking but in the presentation. The pudding trolley in the average British restaurant looks about as enticing as day-old gravy.

Michael Barry's recipes, on the other hand, while quite simple to make, are full of appeal and contrast. So now we crave your indulgence for some dishes that are a bit naughty – but very nice.

PUMPKIN PIE
Serves 6

Pumpkin Pie is the classic American dish for Halloween; All Hallows Eve, the night before All Saints, when ghosties and ghoulies are supposed to be about. The American traditions that go with Halloween ('Trick or Treat' and face lanterns from hollowed-out pumpkins) seem to be catching on over here, so I hope Pumpkin Pie will as well. It's very rich, golden brown in colour and most resembles our own treacle tart in texture and taste. It doesn't need a whole pumpkin: one slice weighing about a pound (450g) will do fine; you can find pumpkin in many supermarkets and most ethnic food markets.

8 oz (225g) shortcrust pastry (home-made or ready-made)
1 lb (450g) prepared pumpkin, peeled and de-seeded
1 tbspn of molasses
4 oz (110g) soft brown sugar
2 eggs
1 oz (25g) butter
1 tspn of cinnamon
Grated rind of a lemon
2 oz (50g) walnut/pecan nuts (optional)

Line an 8-inch (20.5cm) pie tin with the pastry. Boil the pumpkin in water till it's soft – about 20 minutes if cut into medium-sized cubes. Mash the pumpkin and add all the other ingredients (except the nuts) and fill the pie case. Decorate with the nuts. Bake at 375°F (190°C), gas mark 5 for 35-40 minutes. Check with a skewer to make sure it's baked evenly. Allow to cool for 5 minutes before serving. Do not refrigerate; the pie will go soggy.

INSTANT CHOCOLATE CAKE

This is my, and my family's, favourite chocolate cake. It's dark, yummy and moist, easy to ice and even easier to eat! The method may sound extraordinary but do trust me. It's a technique that a lot of cooks are developing in different ways for a number of cakes. It has a health bonus too: the oil can be polyunsaturated. No hard fat you bake with is ever quite so 'clean' from the saturates point of view. One thing: don't be tempted to use drinking chocolate instead of cocoa – you need the bitter chocolate tang for maximum success.

6 oz (175g) self-raising flour
4 heaped tbspns cocoa powder
1 heaped tspn baking powder
4 oz (110g) caster sugar
1 dspn black treacle
5 fl oz (150ml) sunflower oil
5 fl oz (150ml) milk
2 large eggs
For the filling and topping:
4 tbspns black cherry jam
1 × 12 fl oz (325ml) carton fromage frais (see page 17)
5 oz (150g) carton double cream

Place all the cake ingredients in a food processor and blend together (or you can place them in a large bowl and mix with a wooden spoon). When it has turned dark brown and creamy, divide mixture in half and spoon evenly into two 7-inch (18cm) greased sandwich tins. Bake for 45 minutes at 325°F (170°C), gas mark 3 and then remove from oven and take the cakes out of their tins. Allow to cool.

Meanwhile, beat the fromage frais into the double cream until it is thick. When the cakes have cooled, spread one piece of the cake with jam and top with a third of the cream mixture. Sandwich both halves together carefully. Spread the remaining cream mixture on top and, using a fork, bring up into peaks.

This cake can be refrigerated for up to 24 hours before serving. Do make sure you use the correct size of sandwich tins. The wrong size could lead to either a biscuit or a gooey mess.

CHOCOLATE BROWNIES

Sometimes known as fudge brownies, these cakes are half-way between a pudding and confectionery. They are almost as gooey to cook as to eat, so non-stick baking paper (widely available) is a good idea and saves quite dramatically on the washing-up. They are very tempting but don't cut the squares too big: they're quite filling, too. Unlike most cakes, they can be eaten hot, almost straight out of the oven, but they don't acquire their really tooth-sticking quality until they are cool.

6 oz (175g) butter (or margarine)
2 oz (50g) cocoa
6 oz (175g) soft brown sugar
2 eggs
2 oz (50g) self-raising flour
2 oz (50g) walnuts, chopped

Melt a third of the butter and add the cocoa. Cream the rest of the butter with the sugar. Add the eggs and flour and then beat in the butter and cocoa mixture. Grease and line a 7-inch (18cm) square tin. Mix in the walnuts and pour into the tin. Bake for about 35 minutes at 350°F (180°C), gas mark 4. Leave for 5 minutes and then cut into squares. They can be eaten hot or cold and are often iced, usually before they're completely cool, with a fudge mixture.

If you want to use a food processor for this recipe, melt the cocoa and a third of the butter and then put all the ingredients except the walnuts in and zip for 5 seconds.

ORANGE ALMOND CRUNCH
Serves 4

We often take for granted food that used to be a luxury, and conversely regard as a luxury that which used to be thought of as commonplace. When oranges first arrived in the UK they were highly prized and carefully handled. Now we hardly noticed them, but they do deserve better. The thick-peeled juicy Jaffas; red-skinned blood oranges from Malta; Moroccan navels; Sevilles, the bitter oranges from Spain; even the names are romantic. We really should try treating oranges with a little old-fashioned courtesy again. This dish, simplicity itself to prepare, combines the juiciness and astringence of the orange with the crunch of almonds and the aroma of rose petals, and is especially nice served with single cream. *Make sure* you get culinary, not cosmetic, rosewater – the difference can be dramatic! (The best place to find it is in wholefood shops and Indian, Greek or Turkish grocers.)

4 Jaffa oranges, peeled and sliced ¼-inch (0.5cm) thick
2 tbspns slivered almonds, lightly toasted
1 tbspn rosewater (culinary)

Place the orange slices in a large bowl in concentric layers. Sprinkle the almonds over the top. Pour 1 tablespoon of rosewater over the oranges. Leave to stand for a short time before serving, so that all the juices get a chance to mingle.

ORANGES IN CARAMEL
Serves 4-6

The favourite end to an Italian trattoria lunch is the presentation of the sweet trolley with a Latin flourish. Just as you think you can't eat another thing, you are tempted. For years I have resisted, or at least, diverted temptation by having the Oranges in Caramel. Glowing, golden globes in a dark sauce that is always tart and refreshing, and at its best fragrant and luxurious. So, avoid the excesses of Zuppa Inglese or cheesecake and go for this instead.

(Make sure you stop the caramel cooking when it's light brown or you'll not only have to start again but you'll have an impossible mess to get out of the saucepan.)

4 large oranges, peeled and sliced
The peel (no pith) of 2 oranges
6 oz (175g) caster sugar
1 cup water
1 cinnamon stick

Cut the orange peel into matchsticks. Blanch the peel in boiling water twice. (This is best done pouring the boiling water from a kettle over the peel placed in a deep bowl.) Melt the sugar in a thick saucepan over a medium heat till it bubbles and goes light brown. (It takes about 2½ minutes.) Take from the heat immediately and carefully add the water. Stir to dissolve the caramel, add the cinnamon, oranges and peel and simmer for just 3 minutes. Pour into a serving bowl and chill. Be sure to serve some peel matchsticks with each orange.

ORANGE CHOCOLATE MOUSSE
Serves 4

The association of orange and chocolate is surely one of the greatest gastronomic affairs. The richness of chocolate and the zest of citrus do balance each other magnificently. This mousse is perfect for an intimate late-night supper, but is pretty good for ordinary dinner parties too. It's very simple to make and, despite the smoothness, has no cream in it. Do buy the bitterest chocolate you can: a lot of British 'dark' chocolate is very sweet compared to continental brands, so it's worth checking the chocolate for taste.

Juice and grated rind of 1 orange
4 oz (110g) bitter, dark chocolate
4 tspns butter, unsalted if possible
4 large eggs, separated

Put the juice of the orange into a saucepan, break up the chocolate and melt it gently over a low heat stirring regularly. When it's smooth, add the butter and grated rind. Let the butter melt and then beat the mixture till it's thick. Taking the pan off the heat, stir in the egg yolks and heat briefly until thick again. BE CAREFUL: too much heat gives you chocolate scrambled eggs. Leave to cool. Beat the whites till stiff and fold the chocolate mixture into them. Pour into custard cups or wine glasses and chill for at least 2 hours. Especially nice with crisp, orange-flavoured biscuits.

BAKED APPLES WITH HONEY

This recipe was devised for use in a microwave: it's the kind of dish that microwaves do best, simple and cooked by a steam-bake method. You can, of course, cook the same recipe in a conventional oven, but it will need about 45 minutes cooking and the apples should be stood in a dish with half a cup of water in it. Either way the secret is to use eating *not* cooking apples, and a flower-blossom honey.

Per person:
1 eating apple, cored but not peeled
2 tspns of sultanas
Pinch of ground cinnamon and cloves
2 tbspns of runny honey

With the tip of a sharp knife, cut around the equator of each apple, just piercing the skin. Stand the apples upright in a glass or pottery baking dish. Put the sultanas into the core of each one and then sprinkle with the spice and top with the honey. To microwave, bake 4 minutes per apple (cumulative time: four apples at the same time, 16 minutes). Don't overcook.

Pancakes

There are all kinds of pancakes from all over the world: the idea of a batter mixture spread on a hot griddle is almost universal. The key to geographical differences is the flour and liquid used; maize and water make tortillas in Mexico, wheat and water make Peking pancakes in China. In Europe the most usual flour is white wheatflour, but we add eggs and a variety of liquids: the British use milk and the French use water or fruit juice, for instance. Below are a couple of regional pancake recipes from Scotland and Normandy, but it's worth remembering how adaptable the basic pancake mixture can be. They can be made with orange juice to be eaten with honey and garnished with an orange section, or made with chicken stock and filled with mushrooms and cream.

Basic method
Makes 8

8 oz (225g) flour (plain not wholemeal)
Pinch of salt
1 egg
1 tspn oil
10 fl oz (275ml) liquid (water, milk or flavoured liquid)

Combine the flour and salt, stir in the egg and mix. Beat in the liquid till the consistency is like single cream. Add the oil, stir, and leave to rest for up to 30 minutes. Heat a heavy pan and oil it *lightly*. Pour a ladle of batter into the pan and swirl around. When bubbles appear after 1½-2 minutes, flip or turn and cook 1 minute more. They will keep stacked with greaseproof paper between them.

OAT PANCAKES

Makes 8

My own version of a recipe long traditional both in Scotland and in parts of England, these are filling and deliciously nutty.

4 oz (110g) fine oatmeal
2 oz (50g) self-raising flour
Good pinch of salt
1 tbspn oil or melted butter
10 fl oz (275ml) water mixed with
  2 tbspns plain yoghurt
For the topping:
Heather Honey
1 × 5 oz (150g) carton double cream (lightly whipped)

Mix the oatmeal, flour and salt together, then mix the oil (or butter) and watered yoghurt together. Combine them and stir well. Leave to mature for at least 20 minutes. Drop into pan (by the tablespoonsful), cook for 2 minutes a side and serve with the honey and cream.

Jill's wine recommendations:

The sweet 'dessert' wines are especially designed to accompany puddings. Muscat de Beaumes-de-Venise has made a name for itself in this line, but there are other contestants to consider too, such as Monbazillac and other (unfortified) Muscat wines, such as Samos from Greece.

Marmalade Cake

This is a real store-cupboard cake that is a great family favourite. I cook it in a long loaf tin, rather than a round cake tin: it makes it easier to cut and allows one of the ultimate self-indulgences, lightly toasted marmalade cake spread with a little butter at tea time. ...

Don't be tempted, by the way, to add more marmalade – it sinks to the bottom and doesn't help a lot.

4 oz (110g) butter or soft margarine
8 oz (225g) self-raising flour
1 tspn baking powder
3½ oz (90g) caster sugar
2 eggs
Grated rind and juice of 1 orange and 1 lemon
3 tbspns marmalade

If you've got a food processor, you can put all the ingredients into it (except the marmalade) and make the cake in 30 seconds. If mixing by hand, make sure the butter or margarine is soft, then beat *all* the ingredients together with a wooden spoon till creamy. Pour into a non-stick 2 lb (900g) loaf tin and bake for 45-60 minutes at 375°F (190°C), gas mark 5, until a skewer pushed into the middle comes out clean. Cool on a rack for at least 3 hours before eating.

CLASSIC BAKED CUSTARD
Serves 2

This is one of those dishes that somehow have nursery or invalid connotations, quite undeservedly. It is light, subtle and delicious, and using the semi-skimmed milk now on sale everywhere, it can be relatively low in fat. Traditionally, it's cooked in a pan on the top of the stove, but I prefer to cook it in an oven. A pretty dish means you can serve it directly on the dining table.

2 eggs
10 fl oz (225ml) milk (semi-skimmed if possible)
1 oz (25g) caster sugar
½ tspn vanilla essence
½ tspn nutmeg, grated

Warm the milk and beat the eggs with the milk, sugar and vanilla. Pour (through a sieve) into a 1-pint (570ml) soufflé dish, sprinkle with nutmeg and place the dish on a baking tray with 1 inch (2.5cm) of hot water in it. Bake at 300°F (150°C), gas mark 2, for 40-50 minutes until golden on top and set to a jelly. Cool and refrigerate for 2 hours before eating.

BREAD BASKET

My grandfather was a baker. He had a small split-level bakehouse at Winnington in Cheshire. The sacks of flour were stored on the ground floor, and the great oven was in the room above, up a set of open-tread steps. When I picture it, and remember breathing in that glorious promise of hot crusty loaves, I see only white bread. How astonished my grandfather would have been at the brown revolution.

The statistics show that, as a nation, we're eating five times as much brown bread in the eighties as we were in the seventies. The reasons for its rise in popularity are twofold. Firstly, it's now widely accepted that fibre is essential in a healthy diet; we're more health-conscious and we know that brown bread has a much higher fibre content than white. Secondly, we're putting a greater premium on taste, and good brown bread is rich in flavour. As a result we've come to believe that brown is beautiful.

Demand has spawned bewildering variety. In a recent survey, we counted 58 different types of brown loaf on offer (and that total doesn't include a piebald confection made by a Somerset baker, which is brown at one end and white at the other!)

Acknowledging that the wide choice of loaves presently available could easily be a recipe for confusion, the government has introduced three specific categories. Look out for these terms in the shops; don't be taken in by how brown the bread is – unfortunately, caramel colouring is perfectly legal.

Wholemeal If a loaf has 'wholemeal' in its name, the flour used must be made of wholewheat grain, with nothing removed. Wholemeal bread is the one that's naturally highest in fibre, containing around 8½%.
Brown Under the new regulations, 'brown' isn't just a generic term, it defines a loaf which may be made of a mixture of flours but which must contain around 5% of wheat fibre (sometimes known as bran), which is the brown covering of the grain, underneath the shell.
Wheatgerm Again, whatever the flour used, the baker must add a specific amount of nutritious wheatgerm, the vitamin-rich part of the grain. The fibre content of this loaf is around 4½%

Although brown has become established as the most fashionable colour in the bakery, that's only part of the story. The more significant underlying trend is towards widely available, nutritious, freshly baked bread, brown or white, in a mouth-watering range of shapes, textures and flavours. Hot Bread counters in supermarkets and shops are now commonplace, and the small bakery is enjoying a remarkable revival. In other words, at last they're giving us what we want.

The cheeriest news of all, however, is that, for a growing band of bakers, like Stephen Harrell-Bond, whom I met at the Oxford Bakery and Brewhouse, this is just the beginning. A young Californian who trained at the National Bakery School in London, Stephen believes we can best make progress by combining the latest know-how with traditional techniques. Aware above all of his responsibility to the consumer, he's concerned with quality rather than cosmetics. Linking with the tiny brewhouse on the premises, he was using brewers' yeast just as bakers did 150 years ago. Stephen prefers ingredients which contain as few additives as possible; not because he believes additives are harmful but because, he argues, we don't yet fully understand them. The more simple the approach the more sure he can be of what goes into his loaves. I can only add that the proof of his philosophy is in the chewing – his is some of the best bread I've ever tasted.

Whether it's brown or white, good bread can be very versatile, as we're about to discover. Take that much underrated snack, the sandwich, for instance. You'd never know it to judge by the average British Rail buffet, but there's an infinity of fillings and toppings which can transform a loaf into a really different, tasty, cheap and wholesome family meal. And for connoisseurs of bread and butter pudding, we reveal the secrets of Anton Mosimann's definitive version, as served at the Dorchester.

SODA BREAD

Soda bread is often thought of as a poor relation to yeast-risen bread,
but it isn't. It's different, both in texture and taste, more spongy –
particularly the white version – slightly sweeter and a lot less laborious.
These two versions are great as alternatives to traditional bread: they
are best eaten the same day, if possible while still warm from the oven.
Do remember, that baking *soda*, used in the first recipe, is different from
baking powder, used in the second.

WHITE SODA BREAD
Makes 1 loaf

1½ lbs (700g) unbleached white flour
1 tspn each: baking soda, cream of tartar, salt
10 fl oz (150ml) milk and water, mixed in equal quantities

Mix all the dry ingredients together thoroughly. Pre-heat the oven to
475°F (240°C), gas mark 7. Add the milk and water to the flour and salt
mixture. Knead lightly for 1 minute until they are thoroughly blended.
Shape into a large round ball and place on a greased baking sheet. Slit
the top of the dough (to pattern it) and cover with a pudding basin big
enough not to touch the dough. Bake for 30 minutes, take off the basin
and bake for a further 10 minutes till the loaf sounds hollow when
tapped on the bottom.

BROWN SODA BREAD
Makes 2 small loaves

1¼ lbs (550g) wholemeal or granary flour
2 tspns baking powder
1 tspn salt
1 tspn cooking oil
10 fl oz (275ml) buttermilk (or water and natural
      yoghurt mixed in equal quantities)

Mix all the ingredients into a dough quickly but thoroughly. Then
simply divide the mixture into two equal-sized, round loaves and place
on greased baking tray. Bake at 450°F (230°C), gas mark 8 for 30-40
minutes. Tap the bottom: it'll sound hollow when done. Cool on a grid.

Sandwiches

Only too often, sandwiches are last-minute concoctions put together without any special care or thought. This is a real pity because we eat more and more sandwiches in our busy lives, and they really benefit from a little care and fresh ingredients. Here are two traditional ones with a little twist and two unexpected combinations, that make use of some of the delicious breads so widely available now.

Wholemeal Baps with Egg and Cress
Makes 4

Ideal for school lunch-boxes or a quick, delicious snack lunch. This has a double twist on the classic egg and cress: added texture from the hard-boiled egg, and bite from the peppery watercress.

3 eggs
1 tbspn butter
1 bunch watercress, chopped
2 tbspn real mayonnaise
4 wholemeal baps, buttered

Hard-boil one egg and then cool, shell and chop it. Scramble the other two eggs in the butter and add the hard-boiled egg and the mayonnaise. Leave to cool. Add the watercress to the egg mixture, divide into four and fill the split and buttered baps.

Chopped Herring on Black Rye
Makes 4

An unexpected combination – black rye bread looks very dark but tastes quite mild. Chopped herring pâté from delicatessen counters looks grey and bleak but has a lively, spicy taste.

4oz (110g) chopped herring pâté
1 crisp eating apple
8 slices black rye bread, buttered

Divide the herring mixture into four and spread four buttered slices of bread with it. Core the apple and slice into thin rings. Place on top of the herring mixture and cover, pressing gently together before slicing into strips to eat.

CHEESE AND SALAMI ON GRANARY
Makes 4

This is a really filling sandwich with bags of flavour and staying power: I find them ideal for car journeys and travelling lunches of all kinds. My favourite salami is the very garlicky Kosher and a good cheese to use is Gruyère, though you can use other kinds and flavours if you prefer.

8 slices granary bread, buttered
4 slices cheese (Gruyère or Cheddar)
8 thin slices salami, rind removed
4 lettuce leaves
1 tbspn mango chutney

Place the cheese on four of the bread slices, then the lettuce leaves, and two slices of salami on each. Spread with chutney, top with bread and press together firmly.

HUNTERS' LOAF

This was supposed to have been a traditional pocket lunch for French hunters, always careful to look after the inner *homme* even when at *la chasse*. Even if you don't hunt, find an excuse to make this sandwich. It's scrumptious, travels well and can satisfy the most voracious appetites. Don't neglect to 'press' it as directed: it does makes a lot of difference.

1 French loaf
3 tbspn grain mustard
2 large pickled gherkins, thinly sliced
1lb (450g) entrecôte (or porterhouse) steak
1 tbspn salt

Cut the loaf in half lengthways, so you have two 'canoes' of bread. Scoop out and discard some of the crumb. Heat a dry pan till it's very hot. Sprinkle it with the salt and cook the steak 1½ minutes on one side, and then turn and grill 2½ minutes more. Cut the steak into strips to fit the bread. Spread the lower half of the loaf with the mustard (no butter) and put the steak in, covering with slices of gherkin. Cover with the other half loaf, wrap in foil and press under telephone directories or some other weights for 2 hours. To eat, slice it into 2-inch (5cm) pieces.

Garlic and herb croûtons

Croûtons are one of nicest and cheapest ways of turning even an ordinary soup into something special. Be careful not to overcook: they go on browning out of the pan. You'll find that different types of bread go with different flavours of soup – test them first; strong soups are best with brown bread croûtons, delicate ones with white.

4 slices white or brown bread, ½ inch (1 cm) thick
4 tbspns cooking oil (sunflower is best)
1 tspn garlic salt
1 tspn mixed dried herbs (basil, thyme, chives)

Cut the crusts off the bread then slice bread into ½-inch (1cm) fingers; then across into ½-inch (1cm) cubes. Heat oil in a pan big enough for them to make a single layer. Add the cubes and turn every 30 seconds for 2-3 minutes over a medium heat. When they are golden, take out and drain on kitchen paper. While still hot, sprinkle with the herbs and garlic salt. They will stay crisp for 12 hours, but are best hot.

Toasted cheese in four disguises

The English call it Welsh Rarebit, the Welsh call it Caws Enllyn and the French call their version Croque Monsieur. Whatever it's called, it's loved everywhere and now, with the variety of breads, cheeses and relishes that are available, the changes that can be rung make this quick snack a meal in its own right.

Cheddar and anchovy toast
Makes 4

4 slices granary bread
8 slices Cheddar cheese
1 standard-size tin anchovies in oil

Toast the bread on one side only. Place the cheese (two slices per piece) on the untoasted side, place two anchovy fillets in the shape of a cross over each and toast till the cheese bubbles.

PITTA AND HALOUMI
Makes 2

A Middle-Eastern version of cheese on toast, using pitta bread and a white, salty cheese which melts most satisfactorally. You can use other cheese but Haloumi is worth seeking out in delicatessens.

2 pitta
4 oz (110g) Haloumi, thinly sliced
8 black olives, stoned

Heat the pittas for about 2 minutes under a medium-hot grill and then split lengthways along one edge into halves. Lay the Haloumi on the inside surface of the pittas and dot the olives over the cheese. Grill until the cheese bubbles and the bread is just beginning to scorch. Eat hot.

FRENCH TOAST
Makes 2

2 tbspns Dijon mustard
6 oz (175g) Gruyère cheese, grated
½ French loaf

Mix cheese and mustard together. Split the loaf lengthways and toast the crust sides for 1½ minutes until they are hot. Spread mixture on the cut side of the bread, covering it all carefully. Grill until the cheese mixture is melted and golden.

STILTON AND MANGO TOASTS
Makes 4

A new style with the classic combination of cheese and chutney. You can use other blue cheeses, but Stilton has that special bite.

4 slices good white bread
4 tbspns mango chutney
8 oz (225g) Blue Stilton

Toast and butter each slice normally. Spread one side of each slice with the mango chutney. Crumble the cheese and spread over the chutney. Press gently down and then grill the toasts until the Stilton melts and begins to bubble.

ANTON MOSIMANN'S BREAD AND BUTTER PUDDING
Serves 6

In case you thought bread should be reserved for ordinary meals or used as a background or a filler, this recipe will change your mind. Anton Mosimann, the Master Chef at the Dorchester, first began his interest in British cooking some years ago, and despite his many triumphs since then, for many of us his Bread and Butter Pudding is the ultimate revelation of how skill and insight can totally transform the most pedestrian ingredients. Just try it!

9 fl oz (250ml) milk
9 fl oz (250ml) double cream
A pinch of salt
1 vanilla pod
3 eggs
5 oz (150g) sugar
3 small bread rolls, thinly sliced and buttered
1 oz (25g) butter
½ oz (10g) raisins, soaked in water
3 oz (75g) apricot jam
A little icing sugar

Bring the milk, cream, salt and vanilla pod to the boil. Mix the eggs and the sugar together. Add the simmering milk and cream. Pass the mixture through a sieve. Arrange rolls in a buttered, ovenproof dish and add the soaked raisins. Add the milk mixture, dot the remaining butter on top and poach in a low oven at 375°F (190°C), gas mark 3 for 35-40 minutes in a bain-marie (or a tray lined with newspaper and half filled with water). When golden brown on top, dot with apricot jam and dust with icing sugar.

Jill's wine recommendations:
Rosés, well chilled and kept cold in a cool box or wrapped in newspaper soaked in cold water, are perfect picnic/snack wines. This is where the brand Mateus Rosé really comes into its own. Or, for a slightly drier wine, go for Tavel. The Hunter's Loaf deserves a delicious red wine, but you may not want to spend too much on wine for a picnic, so try the French VDQS Corbières or the lighter Minervois.

CHEESE AND CHUTNEY

CHEESE

Food and Drink asked Egon Ronay to cast a critical eye over the cheese offered for sale in London supermarkets. He was not impressed, and there's absolutely no reason to suppose that his reaction would have been any different outside the capital. His first complaint was that, for the most part, the cheeses looked awful; ugly blocks better suited to a building site than a food outlet. Egon also found that, in general, the taste was disappointing, ranging from bland to downright soapy. Even cheeses with an agreeable flavour would have had much more if they hadn't been cut and packed far too young. Worst of all, where were the Great British Cheeses? He found few in evidence and those he did discover were often dismally presented. Egon was also irked by the fact that supermarket customers are rarely allowed to taste the cheese they're thinking of buying. Supermarkets sell most of their cheeses pre-cut and pre-wrapped because it saves on labour; too young because it minimises the expense of storage; and bland because, they argue, that is what the customer wants. Well, it just won't do. Blind tastings suggest that most of us prefer our cheese flavoursome and mature, and if that's the way we like it, that's the way supermarkets will sooner or later have to serve it; even if it does mean extra staff who've been trained to know at least something about what they're selling. It's up to us to insist on choice and quality. Who would think, to look at the cabinets in the average supermarket, that despite numerous setbacks the UK has a wealth of superb farmhouse cheeses?

Fortunately, the battle is far from lost. Our native cheeses, and cheese-makers, have an indefatigable champion: Patrick Rance. He's an ex-soldier who, in 1954, decided that 'it might be amusing, even profitable, to run a village shop'. Via a small advertisement in the *London Standard*, he found and bought Wells Stores in the attractive Berkshire village of Streatley-on-Thames. The problem of what, if anything, to specialise in was easily solved. The youngest son of a parson, Pat counts among his earliest memories the 'pleasurable flavour' of Cheddar cheese. Marketing his favourite food, however, wasn't going to be easy. When he took over the business in Streatley he inherited only 'Danish Blue, Edam and New Zealand Cheddar'.

Opportunities to expand the enterprise began to appear when cheese finally came off the wartime ration. From then on, 'wherever we went, we always explored for cheese. I was very proud when I could put more than 10 different types in the window.'

Now, three decades later, Wells Stores offers an amazing choice; well over 200 different types of cheese, including around 90 unpasteurised farmhouse cheeses made in the UK, all in magnificent condition. Managed by Pat's son Hugh, the shop now supplies restaurants and private customers from Padstow to Glasgow, numbering among its clients Egon Ronay and Anton Mosimann. Pat Rance, with his monocle, eyebrows ready for take-off and his kindly twinkle, is a passionate connoisseur. It genuinely hurts his feelings to see supermarkets and other retailers fobbing us off with oddly shaped, tasteless, ill-kept substances which don't really deserve to be called cheese at all. His authoritative work *The Great British Cheese Book* is both erudite and crusading, as well as being a comprehensive guide.

Thanks in no small part to Pat Rance's lifetime campaign, production of British farmhouse cheeses, unpasteurised and distinctive, is enjoying a heartening revival. Just prior to the Second World War there were 1600 farms in the UK making traditional cheeses. Those days are fondly remembered by a friend of mine, then a farmer's wife, who used to hang her Cambridge-made cheeses under Magdalene Bridge where it was cool and humid, though somewhat vulnerable to passing punters.

With the outbreak of war, farmhouse cheese production came to a full stop. By 1982, the figure had slowly picked up again to around 130 farms, dairies and creameries making traditional cheeses, and it has since rapidly accelerated to 200 and more. Broadly speaking, they divide into those who make traditional cheeses in their traditional areas (for example Lancashire and Cheshire); those who've revived traditional cheeses after a period of non-production (Cotherstone); and those who've created 'originals' (such as Bonchester). Just as public demand forced brewers and bakers to reintroduce 'real ale' and wholemeal bread, so that same inexorable pressure is ensuring an ever-growing market for Great British Cheese. The difficulty is that, at the moment, they're in relatively short supply and not enough shops outside London sell them. Pat Rance's book, mentioned earlier and available in paperback, has a list of stockists. Meanwhile, if you'd like a short (16–page) guide to British cheeses, send a postal order for 60 pence, including postage (made payable to Wells Stores) to:

Wells Stores
Oxford Rd
Streatley-on-Thames
Nr Reading
Berkshire RG8 9HY

The Milk Marketing Board has also published a directory of farmhouse cheese-makers, although, unlike the Wells Stores list, it obviously only includes those who use cows' milk. (The most rapid growth has been in the number of cheese-makers using goats' and ewes' milk). The directory has details of where and how the cheeses are made, and in what sort of quantities. There's a 50 pence charge, which includes postage. Cheques or postal orders should be made payable to the Milk Marketing Board. The address for that is:

Public Relations Dept.
Milk Marketing Board
Thames Ditton
Surrey KT7 0EL

There isn't room in this *Food and Drink* book for more than the merest hint of the delights in store for the newcomer to Britain's traditional regional cheeses, so I've imagined a map of the country and randomly chosen only eight to act as representatives. They're simply meant to serve as an introduction: I'm happy to say there are plenty more where they come from.

Bonchester From John Curtis' farm near Hawick. The same size and general shape as Camembert, but thinner: has a white, mould-ripened crust. Inside is the colour of rich Jersey cream. Can be enjoyed young and has a different flavour from any other soft cheese.

Cumberland Farmhouse Until Caroline Fairbairn arrived on the scene there hadn't been a decent cheese made in Cumberland for years. She now makes both cows' milk and goats' milk cheeses. The cows' milk variety is an absolutely wonderful hard cheese with a classic, unpasteurised flavour (derived, I'm told, from the Cumbrian coastal plain). Good grilled, too.

Appleby Farmhouse Cheshire Made with unpasteurised milk from Friesian cattle. Rich, crumbly and delicious. The only unwaxed, cloth-bound Cheshire you can buy. (Cloth-binding, as opposed to wax, helps the cheese breathe and mature).

Llangloffan A superb cheese to order for Christmas – or indeed any time. Made from unpasteurised Jersey milk in Pembrokeshire by Leon Downey, a former viola player with the Hallé Orchestra. Leon has fought resolutely against the frustrations of the milk quota, which has prevented him and fellow farmhouse cheese-makers from matching supply to demand.

Single Gloucester Produced from Gloucestershire pastures by Charles Martell. Includes milk from rare Old Gloucester cattle and has a lovely creamy, clean taste. One version has a layer of nettles in the middle, as did the original. Makes an excellent present; can be bought at Cirencester market (among other places).

Three Shires Made at Castle Ashby in Northamptonshire by Jillian Woodford. She wanted to specialise in goats' milk cheese and asked for Pat Rance's advice. He said 'go to France', which Jillian did. She now makes a number of goats' milk cheeses, which Pat rates as highly as any from across the Channel. Me too.

Beenleigh From green and pleasant South Devon. Beenleigh Blue (ivory-coloured with blue in it) is made from ewes' milk. The one I tasted was eight months old, distinctive and full of flavour. Also, Harbourne, made from goats' milk; a powerful, creamy cheese, almost sweet at first but with a very positive aftertaste.

Neal's Yard Creameries Cheeses sold at Neal's Yard, a delightful oasis in London's Covent Garden, but now made in Kent. They produce several Coulommiers-shaped cheeses – fresh as opposed to mould-ripened and designed to be eaten young. One has parsley and garlic, another has spring onions and a third is made with pepper. Also the best yoghurt I've ever tasted (well, except in Greece maybe) made with vegetarian rennet.

Now, a brief call to arms: it is up to all of us who value good food to buy 'Real Cheese' wherever possible, and resolutely demand it where not. We really influence the quality of the food we're offered – it worked for beer so why not cheese?

Jill's wine recommendations:
Port and robust red wines, traditionally expected to team with cheese, are certainly not the only alternative, nor even the best. Fuller white wines such as those made from the Chardonnay go well, and, even more of a surprise, so do sweet whites. Essentially, you could continue with anything you have been drinking during the meal.

CHUTNEY

The nicest thing about home-made chutneys (the perfect accompaniment to a piece of 'Real Cheese') is how easy they are. With jam you have to worry about it setting; with marmalade you have to shred the peel; with fruit curds you have to make sure they don't curdle. With chutneys, however, you just stick'em in the pan, cook, add sugar, boil and bottle. And changing flavour or emphasis can be so easy. An ounce of this, a spoonful of that, and another totally original chutney is born. I've suggested two basic recipes: one for apples and one for tomatoes and a few changes or alternative flavours to go with each. Don't be afraid, though, to experiment with your own ideas!

BASIC APPLE CHUTNEY
Makes approximately 8 lbs (3.6kg)

4 lbs (1.8 kg) cooking apples, peeled, cored and chopped
2 lbs (900g) onions, peeled and chopped
1 lb (450g) sultanas
1 tbspn mixed pickling spice
1 pt (570 ml) cider vinegar
1 lb (450g) light brown sugar

Mix apples, onions and sultanas. Wrap the pickling spice in muslin and put the whole lot in a pan with the vinegar. Bring to the boil and simmer gently until the fruit is soft and the sultanas have 'plumped'. (You can leave it for up to 12 hours to mature at this point.) Heat up and stir in the sugar till it dissolves completely, bring to the boil, remove spices and bottle – hot – in sterilised jars. Keep in a cool place for one month before eating.

Variations:
1   Quince. Substitute 1 lb (450g) of peeled and cored quinces (golden, pear-shaped fruit) for 1 lb (450g) of apples; they give a garnet colour and an exquisite scent to the chutney.
2   Ginger. Grate 1 oz (25g) of fresh ginger and use it stirred into the mixture instead of the spice bag: results in a sharp and lively chutney.
3   Apricot. Replace the sultanas with 1½ lbs (700g) dried apricots, quartered. It makes a chunky and mild chutney with a light flavour.

TOMATO CHUTNEY
Makes approximately 8 lbs (3.6kg)

4 lbs (1.8kg) tomatoes, ripe and firm
2 lbs (900g) cooking apples, peeled, cored and chopped
2 lbs (900g) Spanish onions, chopped
4 cloves garlic, crushed
½ tspn chilli powder
15 fl oz (400ml) pickling vinegar
1 lb (450g) caster sugar

Cut up each tomato into eighths. Mix all the ingredients together (except the sugar) and boil for 40 minutes, or until the consistency is thick and jammy. Add the sugar and stir to dissolve, simmer for 10 minutes and bottle in sterilised jars. Keep for two months before eating (if you can bear the delay).

Variations:
1 Peppers. Substitute 2 lb (900g) red and green peppers (diced) for 2 lbs (900g) of tomatoes; makes a jewelled chutney with a bit of crunch.
2 Dark Tomato. Add a tin of concentrated tomato purée to the mixture before cooking and substitute a soft, dark brown sugar for the caster sugar: gives a dark, almost maroon, rich, ketchupy version.

CHRISTMAS

I was fascinated to learn from the New Caxton Encyclopedia that turkey fossils dating back 40 million years have been found in the US. I think I once bit into one of roughly the same vintage in a British Rail dining-car, but I couldn't be sure.

Up to the early nineteenth century, Michael Barry tells me, Norfolk turkeys used to be walked down to London over a period of weeks, in time for the Christmas market. He claims they wore specially made shoes for the trip, or sometimes had their feet dipped in tar. It wasn't April Fool's Day when he passed on this information, and since a fairly recent British film focused on a flock of geese making much the same trek, I'm inclined to believe it.

Nowadays a turkey's last journey is much less picturesque, usually consisting of the short haul to the processing plant. In the UK, we consume more than 10 million turkeys a year, 70% of them frozen, the remainder fresh, and of the fresh market, 5% are free range. They fall into four categories:

Wet Frozen The birds are chilled in water and then frozen (the method used for 99% of frozen birds). If there's more than 5% of water added to the weight of the turkey, then, by law, water must be mentioned on the list of ingredients.

Dry Frozen After being washed, the turkeys travel along a drip-line, so that all the excess water can drain off. Next, they're air-blasted in a special chamber to chill before freezing. You can recognise them by the wrapper, which says 'No added water'. Main producers: Twydales (Buxted are doing some too). When cooked, they don't dry out as much as Wet Frozen birds.

Farmfresh Killed at 18 weeks or over, compared with 12-14 weeks for frozen birds. If the producer is a member of the Traditional Farmfresh Turkey Association, which was established two years ago, the bird will hang for a minimum of seven days and must be dry-plucked. More expensive than frozen turkey, but a superior flavour.

Bronze Top of the range. Prior to the mid-1950s, this traditional breed was the most favoured turkey. Consumers' objections to the black stubble left after plucking (plus demand for volume) led to the development of the modern white turkey (which can be plucked much younger). Raised to maturity in the Farmfresh method with plenty of space and the best food, the Bronze turkey has been bred back to the wild stock. It has a broad breast and incomparable flavour, though it is inevitably more expensive than the rest. It's only available through butchers and even then not everywhere. Derek Kelly Turkeys Ltd of Danbury in Essex, who've pioneered the revival of the Bronze bird and are the major producers, promise a more plentiful supply for Christmasses in future. (It's no good writing to them because they aren't yet geared to cope with direct-sell to the public.)

I've gone on at some length about the Bronze turkey for two reasons: it's the best-tasting bird, by common consent, and its increasing popularity is in line with the overall movement towards recapturing freshness, flavour and character in food. At the same time, it can't be denied, of course, that frozen turkey does indeed represent very good value for money.

Meanwhile, we have to bear in mind that, whether frozen or fresh, turkey (like chicken) may be host to salmonella and should be treated in exactly the same way as that described in Chicken I (see page 34). Do remember that it'll take longer to defrost a turkey.

Should you feel like a change for your Christmas meal, you might try mallard or pheasant. The pheasant season runs from 1 October to 11 February. Hen birds are fattier and not as likely to dry out as cocks, but the male has the advantage of being large enough to feed four people. Hang from the neck, so that air can circulate (leaving feathers on and innards in) for about a week in cold weather or three days when it's warmer.

Mallard needn't be hung at all if it's freshly killed. The season for this wild duck stretches from 1 September to 27 February. Prices vary greatly, as they do for pheasant, but it's obviously cheaper to buy in rural areas. Now let's turn to ways of cooking the Christmas feast.

CRAFTY TURKEY ROASTING

It's only fair to admit that, although this is a very healthy way to roast a turkey it was actually designed in order to give you a succulent bird. There is a lot of argument about how long to roast a turkey, some recommendations being twice the time per pound than others. My experience is that this method below shortens the cooking time because the turkey is not stuffed in the body cavity and because of the effects of the steam. There does seem to be a rule that frozen turkeys need a bit longer than fresh ones, even if they have been thoroughly defrosted, and, as Chris wrote earlier, *they must be*. Whatever your choice of bird, try this method and you'll be rewarded with a succulent fowl plus delicious gravy and easy washing-up. What further recommendation could there be?

A few rules:

1   Defrost a frozen turkey for at least 48 hours.
2   Don't stuff the body cavity, only the breast end.
3   Consider a non-meat stuffing. (See page 110 for Sweet Rice Stuffing.)
4   Keep the water topped up (see below).

Place the turkey on a wire rack that will fit inside the roasting pan. Put 1½ pints (900ml) of water under the turkey and squeeze the juice of a lemon over it. Place the lemon pieces in the body cavity, season highly and cover with butter papers or buttered foil to make a tent – not wrapped up too tight. Heat the oven to 350°F (180°C), gas mark 4. Roast the turkey for:

18 minutes to the lb up to 12 lbs (5.4kg) in weight
16 minutes to the lb up to 18 lbs (8.2kg) in weight
14 minutes to the lb above 18 lbs (8.2kg) in weight

Leave to rest for at least 10 minutes while you dish up the vegetables and then pour off the liquid from the pan to use as delicious gravy.

ROAST PHEASANT WITH APPLES
Serves 2-4

If you don't have a large number of people to feed at Christmas, or if you just fancy a change from turkey, pheasant is a good alternative. It's got lots of flavour and — as long as it isn't too high — not that greasy a texture. It's easy to cook and has lots of meat on it, unlike duck. A cock pheasant should feed four and a hen two or three. You can, of course, make delicious pheasant casseroles, but I think the festive season needs a festive roast. Make sure it's been properly hung (see Chris's advice, page 101) and do pre-heat the oven: speed is of the essence.

1 pheasant
½ cooking apple, peeled, cored and chopped
1 sprig of thyme
Salt and freshly ground black pepper
Butter paper
1tbspn redcurrant jelly
1 tbspn double cream

Pre-heat the oven to 425°F (220°C), gas mark 7. Stuff the cleaned pheasant with the apple pieces and thyme. Season pheasant and place a wrap of butter paper over the top.

Put in a casserole and cook for 1 hour (removing the butter paper before the last 10 minutes of cooking).

Take the apple pieces out of the pheasant and put them into a saucepan with the juices from the casserole dish. Add the redcurrant jelly and double cream to the apple mixture. Heat the sauce while stirring until well blended, thick and creamy (you may want to use a blender for smoothness).

Place the pheasant on a dish and carefully spoon the sauce around the edges before serving. As an alternative, the sauce can be served in a gravy boat.

ROAST GOOSE
Serves 6

Our traditional celebration roast (before turkeys arrived from the US) used to be either a sirloin of beef or a roast goose. Beef continues its popularity, but goose has had a cool reception until recently, especially as it's thought to be greasy. It can be, but not if cooked in this way. Goose is rich, however, and a little goes a long way, which is an advantage in a bird that has a high proportion of bone to meat. Try to pick a young goose or even a large gosling, not more than 10 pounds (4.6kg) in weight: anything larger may be a little tough. Serve with a sharp green apple sauce, mashed potatoes and celeriac (see page 66) and red cabbage cooked with a little sugar and vinegar.

10 lb (4.6kg) goose
2 lemons
Salt and freshly ground black pepper

Rinse the goose. Turn upside down and prick the back all over with a darning needle or small skewer. Squeeze one lemon and rub the juice into the skin. Cut the other lemon in half and place in the cavity. Season and place in oven at 350°F (180°C), gas mark 4, breast side down on a wire rack in a roasting pan. It'll need 18 minutes per pound (so a 10 pound (4.6kg) bird, for instance, will need 3 hours roasting). After half-time, turn it over carefully and continue roasting breast side up.

When cooked, pour any juices inside the goose into a pan as the basis for gravy. Let the bird stand for 10 minutes and serve. The (saturated) fat – about 1 pint (570ml) – which is left in the pan can be discarded, but (if you can take the nutritional guilt) it makes the most delicious sauté potatoes.

Jill's wine recommendations:
Game certainly calls for a powerful red wine as an accompaniment – the Syrah grape is itself a little gamey, and so makes a good partner. The better wines from the northern Rhône such as Hermitage and neighbouring Crozes-Hermitage are good examples. Like chicken, turkey can take either red or white. For Christmas dinner, you might want something a little special such as a white Gewürztraminer from Alsace or one of the village-name Beaujolais, such as Fleurie.

TURKEY ROULADE
Serves 6

Turkey left-overs are always a Christmas dilemma, though I must say, turkey and cranberry sandwiches rarely seem to lose their charm with my family. If you fancy something a little more elegant, however, try this delicious and spectacular savoury Swiss Roll, with the left-over vegetables wrapped around the spiced-up turkey chunks. Have courage – it's almost easier to do than read about. It looks good garnished with lettuce, tomatoes and parsley.

2 oz (50g) flour
10 fl oz (275ml) milk
2 oz (50g) butter
1 tspn grain mustard
3 oz (75g) Cheddar cheese
3 eggs, separated
3 oz (75g) left-over stuffing
12 oz (350g) cooked vegetables, chopped
Salt and freshly ground black pepper
1 tbspn Parmesan cheese, grated
For the filling:
8 oz (225g) cooked turkey, diced
3 tbspns milk

Grease an 8½ × 12½ inch (21.5 × 31.5cm) Swiss Roll tin, line with greaseproof paper and grease again. Heat oven to 400°F (200°C), gas mark 6. Put the flour, milk and butter in a saucepan and bring to the boil, stirring continuously. Simmer for 1-2 minutes, stirring until the sauce has thickened. Mix in the mustard and Cheddar and remove from heat. Divide sauce in half and put one half aside. Stir the egg yolks and crumbled stuffing into sauce, together with chopped vegetables. Season and mix thoroughly. Whisk the egg whites until stiff and gently fold into the sauce and vegetable mixture with a metal spoon. Pour mixture into prepared tin and smooth over surface. Sprinkle with Parmesan cheese. Bake for 20 minutes until well risen and golden. Meanwhile, add turkey and 3 tablespoons of milk to remaining sauce and heat through, stirring gently. Spread the turkey mixture on the roulade and roll up carefully along the *long* edge, like a Swiss Roll. Two big spatulas help.

LOW-FAT CHRISTMAS PUDDING
Serves 4-6

In the search for the yummy but healthy Christmas, the low-fat Christ-mas pudding plays an important part. In fact, except for the oils inherent in some of the ingredients (such as the nuts and milk), it's a *no*-fat pudding, as there is no suet, butter or oil added. It produces a deliciously dark and fruity pudding with the authentic Christmassy taste, but not the leaden weight, of the traditional kind. It responds well to being flamed with rum or brandy and can be re-heated very suc-cessfully. What it doesn't take kindly to is long storage. It's mature after a week and unless kept in very dry, cool conditions can develop mould within one month. Best made in December, therefore, ideally a week or two before Christmas and kept in a airtight container. (You can buy traditional Christmas pudding moulds, by the way, from Boots' Cookshops. They'll give you a spherical and truly Dickensian pudding.)

1 lb (450g) wholemeal breadcrumbs
8 oz (225g) currants
8 oz (225g) sultanas
4 oz (110g) apples, grated but not peeled
4 oz (110g) bananas, chopped
4 oz (110g) brazil nuts, chopped
8 oz (225g) soft brown sugar
Juice and rind of 1 lemon
3 tspns of mixed spice
1 oz (25g) almonds, chopped
3 eggs
10 fl oz (275ml) milk
1 tspn salt

Mix together all the ingredients and stir well. Put the mixture into a greased pudding basin, and cover securely with greaseproof paper. The quantities given make enough for one 4-pint (2.3 litre) basin or two 2-pint (1.1 litre) basins. Steam for 3 hours and then allow to cool. Store in a cool, dry place until Christmas Day and then steam for 1 hour, before serving in the traditional way.

LOW-FAT MINCEMEAT/MINCE PIES
Makes 7 lbs (3.18kg)

The dietary problem with low-fat mince pies isn't, surprisingly, the mincemeat: the recipe below, for instance, creates wonderful, completely fat-free mince. The problem is the pastry. There is a pastry made without shortening called Greek (or Turkish) Filo, which has no fat in it, although it's usually cooked with butter. Unfortunately, none of the substitutes taste anything like real flaky pastry, even if the filling is authentic on the palate. The only suggestion that seems to make sense is to make pastry with half the normal quantity of fat you might usually use and to roll it very thin. Top the pies with a dollop of meringue mixture rather than more pastry. It doesn't cut out the fat altogether, but it does reduce it dramatically. This recipe makes 7 pounds (3.18kg) of mincemeat and keeps up to 3 months in a cool, dark place.

1 lb (450g) soft dark sugar
15 fl oz (400ml) apple juice
4 lb (1.8 kg) cooking apples, peeled and cored
1 tspn allspice
1 tspn powdered cinnamon
1 lb (450g) currants
1 lb (450g) raisins
4 oz (110g) slivered almonds
Grated rind and juice of 1 lemon

Melt the sugar in the apple juice. Chop the apples into small pieces and, when the sugar is completely dissolved, add the apples and all the other ingredients. Bring to the boil and simmer for 30 minutes until it all blends together in a soft mash. Bottle in sterilised jars when hot! Put greaseproof discs on top and tighten seals when cool.

CHOCOLATE TRUFFLES
Makes approximately 14 oz (400g)

And now, after a really healthy Christmas, the moment of self-indul-gence you craved. Make these the week before Christmas, keeping them hidden in the fridge, otherwise they'll never last till the appointed day. They are better than anything you can buy, cheap to make and part of our wish for your Happy Christmas.

12 oz (350g) plain chocolate
1 oz (25g) butter (unsalted)
1 oz (25g) ground almonds
3 egg yolks
2 tbspns double cream
Rind of an orange
Possible coatings:
2 tbspns cocoa powder *or*
2 tbspns icing sugar *or*
2 tbspns ground almonds *or*
2 tbspns chocolate Hundreds and Thousands

Stir all the truffle ingredients in a saucepan and heat gently. When the mixture has blended into a smooth consistency, remove from heat and pour onto a plate. Place in fridge for 1 hour. Sprinkle about 2 table-spoons of *either* cocoa powder, icing sugar, ground almonds or choc-olate Hundreds and Thousands onto a Swiss Roll tin. After 1 hour, remove chocolate mixture from the fridge, scoop a teaspoon at a time of the mixture and roll it into a ball. Then roll each ball thoroughly in one of the coatings. Place the chocolates in paper casings and chill for at least 1 hour before eating. Best eaten within 2-3 days.

Jill's wine recommendations:
The higher quality German wines (Spatlese, Auslese etc) are delicious with traditional Christmas sweets, or to end the meal on a sparkle, Asti Spumante is also an excellent choice.

MADHUR JAFFREY'S CHRISTMAS RECIPES

When Madhur Jaffrey, the famous Indian actress and cook developed these recipes and presented them on *Food and Drink,* she explained that none of them were authentic Indian dishes in their own right. All of them, however, used principles of spicing and flavouring that were entirely Indian. The rice mixture was used to stuff a turkey, but can be cooked separately. If you care to leave out the turkey altogether you will have a most delicious vegetarian, and indeed vegan, Christmas lunch.

Madhur emphasised quite strongly that it is important to get fresh spices if you can and preferably whole ones, not ground up, as they keep better. Many of the spices are now available at Indian grocers throughout most of Britain: your local Tandoori restaurant might help you if you still have a problem finding them. Whatever you eat for Christmas, do try the stupendous potato recipe.

FRIED POTATOES WITH FENNEL SEEDS
Serves 6-8

2 lbs (900g) potatoes
Vegetable oil (enough for about ¼ inch or 0.5cm
    in the bottom of a large frying-pan)
1 tspn fennel seeds, whole
½ tspn paprika
⅛-¼ tspn cayenne pepper (optional)
Salt and freshly ground black pepper

Boil the potatoes and let them cool completely. Peel and cut them in half, lengthways.

Heat the oil in a large frying-pan over a medium flame. When very hot, put in the fennel seeds. A second later, put in the potatoes (cut side down) in a single layer. (If your pan is not large enough, you may need to do this in two batches.) Let the potatoes turn a rich, reddish-brown colour on the bottom before turning them over to brown the second side. Just before the second side is done, sprinkle with the paprika and the cayenne pepper, if you're using it.

Remove the potatoes with a slotted spoon and drain on paper towels. Dust with seasoning and serve hot and crisp.

TURNIPS COOKED WITH TOMATOES AND CUMIN SEEDS
Serves 6-8

2 lbs (900g) turnips
3 tbspns vegetable oil
1 tspn cumin seeds, whole
12 oz (350g) tomatoes, coarsely chopped
15 fl oz (400ml) chicken stock
Salt to taste
¼ tspn ground turmeric
¼ tspn cayenne pepper

Peel the turnips and cut them into quarters (or sixths, depending on size), lengthways.

Heat the oil in a large pot over a medium-high flame. When hot, put in the cumin seeds. After 10 seconds or so, add the turnips and tomatoes. Stir for 1 minute. Add the stock, salt, turmeric and cayenne pepper and bring to a simmer. Cover, turn heat to low and simmer gently for 15-20 minutes until turnips are tender.

Just before serving, heat up the turnips in the liquid, lift them out with a slotted spoon and place on a warm serving-dish. Turn the heat up and reduce the liquid until you have only about 5 fl oz (150ml) left. Pour this over the turnips and serve.

SWEET RICE WITH SAFFRON AND ORANGE RIND STUFFING
For a 9-10 lb turkey (250-275g)

Long-grain rice, measured to the 15 fl oz (400ml)
    level in a measuring jug
2 medium-sized carrots
2 oz (50g) butter (unsalted)
Peel of an orange
7 oz (200g) sugar
2 oz (50g) slivered, blanched almonds
½ tspn leaf saffron *or*
½ tspn yellow (liquid) food colouring
3 tbspns sultanas
¾ tspn salt

Wash the rice thoroughly in a sieve under the tap. Put in a bowl, add 1 quart (50ml) water and leave to soak for 1 hour. Drain and set aside in a sieve over a bowl.

Meanwhile, peel the carrots and cut them diagonally into ¼-inch (0.5cm) slices. Cut the slices lengthways into very thin 'julienne' strips.

Melt the butter in a wide, ovenproof, 3-quart (3.4 litres) pot with a tight-fitting lid over a medium flame. Put in the carrots. Stir and fry for about 5 minutes until carrots are lightly browned. Turn off the heat, remove the carrots with a slotted spoon and set aside. Leave the remaining butter in the pot and set that aside as well.

Cut the orange peel into 2-inch (5cm)-long by ¼-inch (0.5cm)-wide julienne strips. Put them in a pot with 1½ pints (900ml) water and bring to the boil. Immediately drain the orange peel with a collander and rinse under cold water. Repeat this blanching process again and rinse thoroughly at the end.

In a heavy saucepan, combine the orange peel, sugar, almonds, saffron or food colouring, and 5 fl oz (150ml) water. Bring to the boil, and then turn heat down and simmer gently for about 30 minutes, stirring frequently. Add the carrots and sultanas and simmer for another 5 minutes. The peel mixture should be thick and syrupy, rather like melted jam; be careful not to let it burn. Leave this mixure in a warm place.

Heat the oven to 325°F (170°C), gas mark 3.

Put the pot with the butter back on the cooker and heat over a medium flame. Add the drained rice. Stir and fry it for 4-5 minutes, turning the heat down slightly if it begins to catch. Add 1 pint (570ml) of water and the salt. Stir gently and cook until almost all the water has evaporated. Quickly spread the peel mixture over the rice, cover tightly and place in the oven for 25 minutes.

Stir the rice gently before spooning out onto a warm plate. Eat as it is or use to stuff a turkey before cooking.

BRUSSELS SPROUTS AND MUSHROOMS WITH MUSTARD SEEDS AND GARLIC
Serves 6-8

1½ lbs (700g) Brussels sprouts
12 medium-sized mushrooms
3 tbspns vegetable oil
1 tspn black mustard seeds, whole
2 cloves garlic, finely chopped
Salt to taste
5 tbspns chicken stock or water

Trim the sprouts, wash them and pat them dry. Cut each sprout in half, lengthways. Trim the mushroom stems and wipe them with a damp cloth. Cut each mushroom in half, lengthways.

Heat the oil in a large frying-pan (or large wok) over a medium-high flame. When hot, put in the mustard seeds. As soon as the mustard seeds begin to pop (this only takes a few seconds) put in the garlic. Stir for a few seconds until the garlic turns a light brown and add the sprouts. Stir them until they turn bright green. Add the mushrooms and stir for another minute, then add the salt. Pour the chicken stock or water over and cover immediately. Turn heat to medium-low and cook for 7-10 minutes until sprouts are just done (but not mushy). Remove cover and turn the heat up slightly to boil off most of the remaining liquid.

RABBI BLUE'S CHANUKKAH RECIPES

Rabbi Blue, with his warm blend of anecdotes, commonsense and kitchen craft hardly needs much culinary introduction.

The Jewish festival *Chanukkah* (pronounced Honika) comes around at Christmas time: these recipes the rabbi gave us aren't only for that festival, they represent the great tradition of middle-European cooking that Jews of the second diaspora have distributed lovingly across the world. It's by no means the only tradition of Jewish cooking, but – along with chicken soup – Latkes (potato pancakes) and cabbage Borscht must rank high in the hit parade of all-time Jewish favourites. Don't be put off by the extraordinary range of toppings he suggests for the Latkes, by the way; they really are equally good savoury or sweet.

LATKES
Serves 4-6

6 potatoes, chopped
1 onion, chopped
2 eggs
1 tbspn Matzo meal
   (or cracker meal/self-raising flour)
Sunflower oil for shallow frying
Salt and freshly ground black pepper
Possible toppings:
Cinnamon; caster sugar; apple sauce; pickled cucumbers;
   apricot jam; mashed potatoes

Blend the potatoes and onion in a food processor (or grate them if you haven't got one) and drain off liquid: the less liquid there is the lighter the Latkes will be. Mix in the eggs and Matzo meal and stir to form a thin batter.

Heat the sunflower oil in a frying-pan and when it's very hot, drop one or two patties at a time of the mixture into the oil. Fry on both sides until golden brown and crispy.

Remove from pan and drain on absorbent paper. Lay on a dish and serve with chosen topping.

BORSCHT (CABBAGE SOUP)
Serves 6

3 small onions, chopped
1 small white cabbage, shredded
1 green pepper, roughly chopped
1 yellow pepper, roughly chopped
2 tbspns sunflower oil
Knob of margarine
2 level tspns caster sugar
1 × 4 oz (110g) tin tomato purée
1 × 1 lb (450g) tin tomatoes
1 clove of garlic, crushed
1 oz (25g) sultanas
Juice of 2 lemons
1½ pints (900 ml) vegetable stock (cubes can be
    used, but they're not as good)
Extra sugar to taste

Cook onions, cabbage and peppers in the mixture of oil and margarine in a large saucepan. Sprinkle with the caster sugar and continue cooking until browned. Add remaining ingredients apart from lemon juice and, using enough vegetable stock to cover vegetables, simmer for at least 1 hour. Stir in lemon juice and possibly a little extra sugar to taste before serving.

INTRODUCTION TO WINE

Not so long ago, wine was sold only across highly polished mahogany desks by a fairly effete breed of wine salesmen who knew what they were on about. Their customers were even more effete, if anything, and professed to be even more knowledgeable . . . but essentially the world of wine was minute: there wasn't all that much to be knowledgeable about. Only the proven 'classics', the wines with long pedigrees, would ever find their way over here in the first place and you could have been forgiven for believing that no wines were made further east than Bordeaux.

All that has now changed dramatically, however, and the buying and drinking of wine is no longer in the hands of the cellared classes. Two-thirds of all wine is now sold not over a polished desk but via a supermarket trolley. Inevitably, the well-informed wine salesman is virtually a thing of the past, which is regrettable since wine-buyers in the UK – 27½ million at the last count – don't even begin to pretend they know it all. What is badly needed all round, therefore, is simple, constructive help.

You might have noticed that there's already a lot of bumph around on this subject – more has been written about wine in books and articles than you could believe possible – but most of these millions of wise words seem to be directed at the dwindling number of old-fashioned wine-buyers. There are plenty of writers preaching to the élite about expensive fine wines, but little advice available for the new wine-drinkers. Several million people have started buying and enjoying wine since the *Food and Drink* programme began: this section of the book is for those who just want an occasional bottle, getting maximum value and enjoyment for the money.

In a survey we carried out to find out more about the tastes of our viewers (on average 4½ million each week) we discovered that three-quarters of them drink wine every week, and 94% of these 3 million plus will usually spend no more than £3 per bottle. This wine section is designed to offer plain explanations and advice to the 94%. The other 6% are, after all, already more than adequately catered to.

Buying wine is undeniably a much more complicated business than serving yourself with any other item off the supermarket or off-licence shelves. More than 40 different countries now sell their wines widely in the UK, and each of the wines, not just from every country, but from every different area of every country, has a quite different taste and style. Selecting a wine in the right price bracket that you will like, and that will suit your purposes, is quite a skill. Many people new to wine-drinking concentrate on the well-known names, which unfortunately means that they are almost invariably paying more than they need for a less enjoyable wine. Many of the best buys costing up to £3 a bottle are wines *without* a famous name, and finding your way around them is a lot to do with interpreting all the information available on the label – we'll help you do that. In Chapter 2, taking wines country by country, I have tried to untangle the sometimes baffling codes used locally to qualify wine in terms of style and quality.

The A-Z section (beginning on page 145) describes in rather more detail the wines most commonly seen on the shelves. Because there is no consistency in the naming of wines (some have brand names, others are named after places, yet more after grape varieties) this is, of necessity, a somewhat eclectic list. Take the most prominent title on the label and simply look the wine up ... I hope that nine times out of ten you will find it here.

As well as declaring the name of the wine and telling you something about its official quality rating (where one applies), a lot of wine labels offer additional insights into the character of the contents of the bottle ... if you can understand what they are trying to say. Some of these potentially helpful hints are just thrown away, expressed either in a foreign language or in the sort of jargon that is equally difficult to interpret. My aim is that you'll emerge a little wiser when you've read the chapters which follow (even if you never want to use the language of 'winespeak' yourself).

Once you have finally sifted through all the information available, made your choice from all the countless wines on offer and at last got the bottle home, what next? The rudimentary rules about how to serve wine are pretty well known, but how many must be strictly observed? Wine is a living thing, and, like 'Real Ale' or 'Real Cheese', it has a life of its own and is vulnerable to all sorts of outside influences. Within reason, the way you treat it between shop shelf and glass can have quite a drastic effect on how good or indifferent the wine will taste. For this reason, I have outlined what I consider to be the essential 'no-nonsense' rules, designed to get the best results possible from a glass of red, white, rosé or sparkling wine (see page 160, Serving Wine: A Few Simple Rules).

So here you have it, the Absolutely Basic Guide to Wine, starting, incidentally, with a brief introduction as to what wine actually is and how it is made. You'll find no £100 bottles on the following pages, no mystique and no frills. I hope very much that you will find your way easily around the guide – and enjoy reading some of it – but only as a prelude to deriving maximum pleasure from your next glass of wine.

Before you set out to buy your next bottle, however, may I just make a few suggestions about the best places to shop: there may be some excellent alternatives you haven't yet considered. Supermarkets certainly have the lion's share of Britain's wine business today, and if you have to chase up and down the aisles picking up groceries anyway, it's very convenient to include a bottle of wine every now and again. Handy though supermarkets are, however, the service they provide is far from complete, and I would never recommend anyone to buy exclusively from supermarkets. For a start, you will never find any assistants on hand who can help. Also, as I learnt from a survey we carried out for *Food and Drink*, shelf labelling is not usually that brilliant either, so supermarket wine shoppers can find themselves well and truly left to their own devices. Nor are there any auxiliary services; for parties, for instance: no 'sale or return', no discounts on quantity, no delivery and no glasses for hire. You could also be short-changed in terms of the wine itself, since good wine is a very difficult thing to buy in large quantities. No small grower would ever be able to keep the shelves stocked in every branch of any of the big chains, so a lot of the wine has to come from huge, anonymous co-operatives. You could well find more interesting wines in smaller, independent shops.

During our survey, we found that the service offered by the big high street off-licence chains wasn't much better than that in the supermarkets, even though you might expect it to be. Although there was always someone on hand to look after the till, he often knew precious little about the stock and was therefore unable to be much help to customers.

The old-fashioned wine merchant shops we visited, on the other hand, were positively inspiring places to shop, and contrary to their slightly daunting 'up-market' exteriors, had a lot to offer in the way of help (including the odd free tasting) and a good choice of interesting, inexpensive wines. Wine warehouses, which are now springing up around the country selling bottles of wine by the dozen from barn-like premises (usually a little out of the centre of town) provide a completely different kind of service. Price margins are considerably reduced by the unglamorous premises, tastings of a range of wines are often available free, and the assistants are usually both knowledgeable and approachable.

Although new wine emporia are springing up around the country with encouraging speed, your area might as yet have been missed out. An alternative is to buy your wine through a club. If you want further details, here are the addresses of two of the UK's biggest clubs:

The Wine Society
Gunnels Wood Road
Stevenage
Hertfordshire SG1 2BG

The Sunday Times Wine Club
New Aquitaine House
Paddock Road
Reading
Berkshire RG4 0JY

Many off-licences and wine merchants also run their own wine clubs. The advantages of joining are legion: good wines can be delivered to wherever you live, you receive frequent newsletters and wine lists with advice and there are tutored tastings and special offers.

But however you end up buying your wine, I hope that this basic guide will get you off to a good start.

WHAT IS WINE?

Left to its own devices, the juice of any fruit or vegetable will, in time, ferment and turn itself into wine. Loosely speaking, wine is simply a lightly alcoholic, fermented drink, so you can get rhubarb wine, rice wine, carrot wine, plum wine, crab apple wine – any kind of wine you like. More precisely, however, the word *wine* on its own is universally recognised to mean the fermented juice of the wine-making grape. The particular type of grape used is known botanically as *vitis vinifera*, and is very different from the usual eating varieties. It makes a uniquely complex, many dimensional, infinitely variable drink, which is in quite a different class from the fermented juice of any other fruit.

There has always been a great deal of song and dance made about wine and its many virtues; wine bores can go on about it for hours and I certainly don't want to be another wine commentator prolonging the mystery. So what, in plain language, makes one wine different from – and perhaps more expensive than – another?

How wine is made

Essentially wine doesn't have to be made, it makes itself, because all the necessary ingredients for wine-making are contained within the grape itself. During the process of fermentation (which is spontaneous, as anyone who has ever left a fruit salad hanging around too long will know), yeast works on the natural sugar present in the fruit and converts it into alcohol, giving off carbon dioxide as a bi-product.

You will see a white bloom on the skin of any grape berry, although it shows up more clearly on black grapes. This is the yeast. Inside the berry, the juice is sweet; there you have the sugar. Hanging on the vine, these two ingredients are kept apart by the water-tight skin, but crush the bunch or even a single berry and the two will begin to react together. If the crushed grapes (or just the juice) is left unchilled, the seemingly magical process will start very quickly and not stop until either all the sugar has been converted into alcohol by the yeast or the alcohol level has become so high as to kill off the active yeasts. Not all sweet wines, as you might conclude from this, are terrifically high in alcohol; many, such as the high-quality German wines, combine sweetness with a low alcohol content. To achieve this, the fermentation is stopped artificially before the yeast has completed its job. To make cheaper sweet white wines, any yeasts remaining after the fermentation has stopped will be filtered off before a slug of sweetness is added back to the wine.

As well as yeast and sugar, there are other natural wine-making ingredients present in grapes, contained in the skin and the stalk. If you bite into a grape, the overall sensation is of sweetness, but concentrate on the skin or chew on the stalk and the taste will be tart, making the insides of your cheeks feel puckered and dry. The cause of this strange taste and sensation is tannin, which acts as a preservative. It plays an important role when wines, particularly reds, are destined to be matured before being drunk. Since tannin is rather bitter, care is taken not to allow the skin and stalks which contain it to remain in contact with the pressed juice when making delicate white wines; the skin, stalks and the pips (which are too bitter for any wine) are all filtered off before fermentation. This is not the case with red wines, where a certain amount of tannin is to be encouraged.

Red wines generally have more substance and more 'body' than white wines, and are almost all pretty dry, so the tannin taste is not at odds with the intrinsic flavour. As red wines age, the harsh characteristics of the tannin soften and mellow as well as contributing an important dimension of their own to the wine. If you taste a red wine intended to be aged when it is too young, the tannin is easy to detect, giving the wine a hard, easily identifiable, mouth-puckering edge.

WHAT MAKES A RED, A WHITE OR A ROSÉ

The pulp and juice of almost all of the thousands of different grape varieties is white, no matter what the colour of the skin. White wines, therefore, can be made as easily from black or red grapes as from white. Indeed, most champagnes contain the juice of both colour grapes, although in still white wines it is more usual for white grapes to predominate.

White wines made from only white grapes sometimes say so on the label, and the term used to describe such a wine is 'blanc de blancs', literally translated, 'white of whites': white wine from white grapes. In more exceptional circumstances, a white wine may be made from black or red grapes only, and this is called a 'blanc de noirs' (white of black).

To make a red wine, the skins of red grapes must be left in contact with the crushed grapes and juice during fermentation to give sufficient colour to the wine. In hotter areas, the pigment in the skin becomes more intense under the sun's hot rays, and quickly dyes the wine to a rich, dark purple colour. In cooler climates, the colour is less intense, both in the skins of the grapes and eventually in the wine itself. Red wines are generally made exclusively from red grapes, although there are exceptions to this rule, too. Chianti, for instance, generally contains some white grape juice, or 'must', in the blend.

Rosé or pink wines may be made in one of two ways. In most cases the skins of red grapes are left in contact with the 'must' for long enough to give the wine an attractive rose-coloured blush. Alternatively, a little red wine may be blended in with white to make it pink, although this only happens with the cheapest rosés and some rosé champagnes. Rosé wines are not different from whites in colour alone. The inclusion of some of the properties of the red grape adds more body and guts to the overall blend.

The object – apart from simply creating a pretty colour – is to 'beef up' the wine slightly, but as you can imagine, this additional body and flavour can act as a smokescreen as well, covering up all sorts of faults in the wine and disguising less perfect components in the blend. Cheap rosé wines, therefore, must be viewed with a little caution.

THE ROLE OF THE WINE-MAKER

Although the juice pressed from freshly picked grapes will make itself into wine of its own accord, a wine-maker will always intervene and control the process to a certain extent, making sure that the wine is as good as it can be. It's not a question of interfering where things are better left alone: although wine makes itself quite readily, it also has the ability to make itself rotten as well.

Although the bloom on a grape's skin contains healthy wine-making yeasts, less desirable wild yeasts and bacteria are usually also present, brought to the grape either by insects, or carried aerobically – that is, by the air. If the wild yeasts are allowed access to the grape juice, the sugar is converted into alcohol much too quickly and the yeasts wear themselves out before the alcohol content is high enough. The partially made wine is then vulnerable to assault from the bacteria, which makes it sour. The wild yeasts and bacteria, therefore, have to be kept out of the process altogether. The principle way of achieving this is to keep the juice or 'must' away from the air, since both wild yeast and bacteria need oxygen to survive This can be done either by conducting the fermentation in a sealed tank or by dousing the 'must' with sulphur dioxide, which feeds on all the local oxygen.

The wine-maker can also regulate the length of the fermentation period by controlling the temperature. As anyone who's made wine or beer at home will know, the cooler the temperature, the longer it takes for the yeasts to complete their job; and broadly speaking, the longer the fermentation period, the more delicate and subtle the resultant wine. Before sophisticated equipment was designed to control the temperature of the 'must' during fermentation, you could predict, as a general rule, that the hotter the wine-making area, the poorer would be the quality of the local wine. Now there is an abundance of new technology available to wine-makers which can overcome most local handicaps and, consequently, the general quality of even the cheapest wines has improved.

But however streamlined and advanced wine-making aids may have become, the end product, wine, can only be as good as the ingredients that go into it. It's like cooking. Essentially, you can't expect perfect results if you use sub-standard ingredients. And where wine-making grapes are concerned, there are a great number of different factors that radically affect quality. The most important, of course, is the variety of the grape, but since grapes consist largely of water, this accounts for only part of it. The water content of grapes is derived from the earth in which the vine plants its roots, so geology plays an important part. And since the critical ripening of the grapes depends on the weather, the situation of the vineyard and the sort of climate it enjoys are other vital considerations as well.

On the face of it, these details may seem far-fetched and remote; further proof that a lot of fuss and nonsense is made about wine. If you are any sort of gardener at all, however, you will know that even, say, a tomato will thrive or wilt depending on exposure to sun, the supply of water and the type of soil. To look more directly at the effect of the elements on the quality and taste of specific fruit, you can simply take apples as an example. From England you get the Cox, a small, highly scented apple with a sweet, strong flavour, which gradually acquires its relatively intense character over a long, slow growing period, with only intermittent bouts of sun. From areas with hotter climates, such as the South of France, you get the comparatively woolly Golden Delicious, which puffs up quickly under ceaselessly coaxing rays of hot sun. As far as flavour and quality are concerned, a lot of sun is altogether too much of a good thing. It brings on the fruit too quickly for it to be able to acquire much in the way of flavour and character.

THE NATURAL ELEMENTS

The structure of the soil varies considerably around the world; not just the topsoil – whether your garden is dominated by loam, lime or clay – but the deep sub-structure of the earth as well. The vine is capable of surviving without much water, so naturally sends its roots many metres into the ground, drawing elements out at all levels, which will directly affect the taste of the grape and its wine.

Although general geological features may be repeated in different countries and different areas, no two regions are precisely alike, and neither are their wines. Different soils, of course, suit different varieties of grapes, and occasionally you get a perfect combination of the two. That, when teamed up with an ideal climate for vine growing, makes for an exceptional wine.

In warm, southerly areas, such as southern Italy and the South of France, vines grow as prolifically and strongly as weeds, and left to their own devices under the baking summer sun, quickly become weighed down with excessive quantities of fruit. For wine-making purposes, however, such fruit is far from the best. The grape sugar level will have climbed too high, making it suitable only for over-alcoholic, characterless plonk, or worse still, merely for industrial alcohol. Modern wine-making technology has, however, overcome some weather problems, and it is now possible for good wines to be made in climatically 'marginal' areas.

So if too much sun is to be discouraged, what then is the ideal? The best yearly weather for most types of grapes and most types of wines goes as follows: a cool (cold even) winter, during which the vines will remain dormant and conserve their energy; a warm, frost-free spring so the vines will bud and flower, and the flowers will 'set' (i.e. start to turn into fruit); then a summer with a certain amount of sun rationed out gradually, so the grapes will grow and develop slowly, concentrating as much flavour and character within the pulp as possible. When it comes to harvest-time in the autumn, dry weather is an advantage of course, because ripe grapes on the vine can easily spoil, and they are best gathered in when it is cool but dry. Since a temperate climate – not unlike our own – is the one most enjoyed by wine-producing vines, you can easily see how wines made in the same area will vary considerably from year to year as the weather varies. This is how 'vintages' come about, and (where fine wines are concerned) accounts for the sometimes considerable difference in price between the same wine made in different years.

Even at the lower end of the price scale, the vintage or date of a wine tells you what to expect, too. Remember the summer of 1984? It was abysmal, not just in the UK but on the Continent as well, so wines made in 1984 in the more northerly areas are liable to have suffered as a result. Many are rather thin, with insufficient fruitiness to give much body, and are rather sharp and acidic as well. Think of tasting unripe fruit and translate the unpleasant characteristics of say, an unripe plum, to wine made in a poor year.

1985, in contrast, was a comparatively good year in continental Europe. Following an extremely icy winter and a rather cool spring (which reduced the size of the crop), a good warm spell came after a cold start and concentrated the flavours magnificently. The result is good wines in slightly short supply.

So the vintage date on the label tells weather-watchers a bit about the quality of the wine, and reveals how old it is as well. This is important information if you are to enjoy wine at its best. As a general rule, whites should be drunk young, a year or two after the vintage date, and reds should be allowed to acquire a bit of maturity before you pull, or 'draw', the cork. Most reds continue to improve for some years after they're made; up to a decade or more for some of the heavier styles. There are of course exceptions to these very broad rules, which will be described in our 'A-Z of Wines' (see page 145). Not all wines, however, declare a vintage date on the label, only those made from the produce of a single year. Labels without a date signify that the wine is made from grapes grown in several years. With the exception of champagne, these are generally the lesser, cheaper wines.

The factors that together determine what a particular wine will be like, therefore, are: the type of grapes used; the make-up of the soil where the vines are grown; the climate (both in general and in particular during the year in which the wine is made); the techniques adopted by the wine-maker; and the age and maturity of the wine when it is drunk.

In the classic wine-making countries, centuries of experience in vine growing and wine production reveal the perfect spots for making particular sorts of wines; the areas where all the God-given factors just happen to be right. It is these precisely defined areas that are responsible for making the most famous, and most expensive, wines.

Prices and prestige are not merely arbitrary: it is simply that, as we have seen, the conditions for wine-making are more suitable in some areas than in others. If one or two of the critical factors are amiss it is bound to reflect directly and noticeably on the quality of the wine, so at the cheaper end of the scale, regrettably, you are never going to find an absolutely classic wine with all its attributes balanced and blended perfectly. What you *can* find, though, is a bargain in the shape of an excellent wine from a new area. Here, the natural factors may be either already perfect or modified and tailored by new technology, to enable a delicious wine to be made which as yet has had little time to be 'discovered' and sought after. As with any of the other luxuries in life, the prices of the best wines are jacked up by that annoying equation of supply and demand: if no-one had any interest in, say, diamonds, they would be cheap; and so it is with the best wines.

'Undiscovered' wines – undiscovered by wine snobs and label hunters, that is – can be surprisingly well priced. You may never get a bargain with a 'known name', but it is comparatively easy, if you know where to look (read on, read on!), to find an excellent and surprising buy.

THE LANGUAGE OF WINE EXPLAINED

At first glance, many of the hundreds of wine labels which confront the shopper in the wine section of a supermarket or off-licence could have been deliberately designed to confuse or mystify. It is not surprising that the familiar names seem the most reassuring, because if you venture into the unknown and opt for something you've never tried, or perhaps even heard of before, how do you know what you are getting? How do you know that you will actually *like* the contents of your £2 or £3 bottle when you get it home and open it?

The fact is that once you have learnt to find your way around them, wine labels give away much more about the contents of the bottle than it may first appear. For a start, EEC wines always tell you something about the wine's quality, in most cases telling you exactly where it officially rates on a scale of excellence: whether it is just ordinary plonk, or has a bit more going for it in terms of style and character; is average, good or special. But because most wines are foreign (not forgetting the limited supplies of our own native English wine, of course) the information is not only expressed in the language of the wine's country of origin, but even more confusingly, in a kind of local shorthand, gradually evolved over the decades to classify each country's wines. This shorthand, however, is easy to interpret, I promise you . . . and I explain how in the following pages. You'll find the terms most commonly used explained in the Glossary (see page 140).

All labels must, by law, tell you a number of bare essentials – such as how much there is in the bottle, for instance. Traditionally, this was usually 75cls (that is, 0.75 of a litre), but most of the cheaper wines now come in 70cl bottles. The country of origin of the wine must also be clearly revealed, along with the name and address of the maker of the wine or company responsible, in case of complaint. Certainly in the past, the scantiest information was all you were likely to get. Wine-makers used to be arrogant enough to believe that their name was all: that any further description of the wine was quite secondary. Who ever heard of a first-class claret boasting anything on the label but the holy name of the priceless château . . .? The right temperature to serve the wine? You must be joking! But such insularity, except where the greatest wines in the world are concerned, is a thing of the past. Now wine-makers and sellers usually try to tell you as much as possible on the label. (The notable exception to this is the fact that the various additives used in production are not declared. That's another story – suffice it to say that recent scandals in Austria and Italy bring the possibility of detailing the contents on the label ever closer.)

So as well as defining more precisely the region in which the wine was produced and declaring the vintage (that is, the year in which the wine was made) if such a date applies (see page 126), you may find a description of the style of the wine on the neck label and a revelation of the alcohol content expressed as a percentage of the whole; say 8% for a mild, dry white, going up to a hefty 14% or so for some beefy reds from the hotter wine-making areas. To qualify as wine under EEC laws, it must have a minimum alcohol content of 7%. (That's about two and a half times as potent as beer, and around a quarter of the strength of spirits.) It used not to be the practice to reveal the names of any grape varieties used in making wine either -- you were just supposed to 'know'; and among the 'classic' wines (and the cheaper blends) the grapes used are still kept a mystery. In a lot of cases, however, it is useful to know what the main ingredients are in a bottle of wine. Once you know what a certain grape type tastes like, you can then confidently go on to try different wines made from the same variety throughout the world. Wines made outside the 'classic' wine-making areas of Europe (that is, made in the less well known spots of Europe, Eastern European countries, North and South America, Australia and South Africa) tend to be labelled clearly with the predominating grape varieties, which is a useful flavour guide increasingly found on wine labels. For instance, Chardonnay is the grape used in classic white burgundy from France, but you won't see the grape's name on the bottle. In other countries, however, wine-makers using the grape are quite likely to call their wine simply 'Chardonnay'.

A number of wine bottles now carry back labels as well, which gives further scope for conveying information. Ludicrously, some wine-makers persist in using the space to perpetuate the 'mystery' surrounding the making and enjoyment of wine, giving a lot of useless data whimsically describing ancient traditions which no longer have any relevance to modern wine-making techniques. The majority, however, now tell you something about the wine itself, suggesting food that would make a good accompaniment and give serving advice. Do turn the bottle round and look out for this.

A very useful code has been devised to identify the dryness or sweetness of wines, a vital piece of information where white wines are concerned. (Most red wines are dry, so they are not classified on this scale.) A number of major – and not so major – supermarket and off-licence chains have adopted the code, and use it either on the front (or back) wine labels themselves, or include it in any description of the wine that appears on the shelf. The code runs from 1 to 9, 1 being as dry a wine as you can get, and 9 indicating the most concentratedly sweet wines. A Muscadet, for example, rates number 1, Liebfraumilch number 5 and Asti Spumante number 7. If you keep in mind a particular wine you have liked, as a point of reference, you can then find another wine that might appeal to you with the same number on the scale.

Although most red wines are much of a muchness on the sweetness/dryness scale (there are exceptions, of course, and these are described in our A-Z on pages 145-59), they do have considerable differences in terms of weight (usually described as body) and in texture. Various wine companies have been working for a while on a code to classify red wines, and the system to be officially adopted is likely to be announced early in 1987 (the *Food and Drink* programme will have the details for you, of course). Victoria Wine have classified their red wines for a while now, calling them 'light bodied', 'medium bodied' or 'big'; and in texture: 'soft' or 'firm'.

PREDICTING QUALITY

A wine is, of course, only as good as *you* think it is, since if you're drinking it you are the one who counts. Nevertheless, most wines are officially rated on some sort of quality scale: EEC countries impose strict tests on all their wines, both in the laboratory and in front of a highly critical tasting panel, and the wines are all legally graded as a result. (The table on pages 138-9 explains the different quality grades for you.)

This is somewhat different from, say, a cookery expert in the Women's Institute judging a class of cakes, where 60% of the marks go on taste, because with wine there is such a complex technical element to be considered as well. Judgement of a wine goes right back to the roots – quite literally – of the vine, taking into account all aspects of geography, geology, methods of viticulture (grape-growing) and vinification (turning the juice into wine); assessing and grading the grapes themselves and the wine they produce. Official grading of a wine's quality is not just concerned with the proof in the glass but the whole history of the vineyard and the wine-making area.

You may well say this doesn't happen with cakes or marmalade or even with gin, so why should it with wine? Is it just another way of baffling the public and perpetuating the mystery? Actually no: it's meant to simplify matters instead. Although you personally may not agree with some of the classifications – perhaps in some instances you actually prefer the taste and style of the more modest wine – in the confusing maze of alternatives confronting you in the wine shop itself, it does give you some guide as to where you are if you know how the wine rates technically (and, more to the point, how wisely you are spending your money). Higher quality is invariably linked with a higher price, and so too should a lower quality status carry a smaller price tag Note I said 'should' . . . but of course things are not always just so; it is worth checking what you are getting before you pay.

In order to classify and pigeon-hole the wines precisely, each country uses its own official quality scale. These scales are all different, of course, but they can be related one to the other, to get some sort of uniform picture (see the chart on pages 138-9).

France

France is well known for famous, classic wines that sometimes fetch the most exhorbitant prices, but being one of the largest wine producers in the world, it is hardly surprising that not all the millions of litres produced there are equally noble. In fact, the bulk are very ordinary, described simply as **Vin de Table**. Wines labelled 'Vin de Table' are likely to be rather bland and unrefined: these are generally unspecified blends of basic wines coming mainly from the south, where the scorching sun encourages the vines to bear massive quantities of high-sugar fruit. The wines can consequently be rather coarse and high in alcohol.

Vin de Pays on the label still denotes a wine of fairly ordinary quality, but this time the wine has more to boast in terms of individual character. Instead of just being 'mass-produced', as many 'Vins de Tables' are, to make a wine qualifying for the 'Vin de Pays' status, the wine-maker has gone to rather more trouble. This is a good type of wine to look out for at the lower end of the price range.

Next up the French scale comes the rather cumbersome title of **'Vin Délimités de Qualité Supérieure (VDQS)**: loosely meaning a wine of superior quality. 'VDQS' wines are still a shade rustic, they do not include any of the famous names, but they are well made and many are delicious in their own way. To earn this title, vineyards and wineries are subjected to tighter controls, and the resultant wine emerges with an identifiable local style. Minervois, for example (from near Narbonne in the South of France) is a 'VDQS', and any Minervois you buy will be the same sort of wine with the same sort of taste and smell. Since it has earned the title, you can guarantee that you won't get a 'rogue' example that you really do not like (that is, if you have established that you do actually like the Minervois style). In a blind tasting, an experienced wine taster should be able to pick out and identify an individual 'VDQS' wine because it has such an obvious and unique personality.

The top quality status in France is **Appellation Contrôlée**, which is the classification used to describe wines that range from being simply good to quite exceptional. An enormous range of wines (25% of the country's total production) displays these words on the label in one form or another, and it is the form the words take which pin-points precisely *how* good the wine in the bottle ought to be. To explain: 'Appellation Contrôlée' actually means that the use of the name of the wine is officially controlled. It's allowed to be used only by wines meeting certain minimum standards laid down by law. In most instances, French wines are named after the area from which they come, so it is the area name that is officially controlled and this is the big pointer to the wine's precise quality, because the more specific the place name that is 'controlled' – say an individual vineyard or château – the better the wine. The huge 'Appellations', referring to a whole wine-making district, such as Bordeaux (written on the label as 'Appellation Bordeaux Contrôlée) are used for the most basic wine made in the area eligible for 'Appellation Contrôlée' status. Slightly better wines would receive the 'Appellation' for, say, a single commune in the area (such as Margaux) and wines that are better still would receive the classification for the actual property where the wine is made.

In addition to pigeon-holing a wine precisely in terms of quality, there are certain 'handles' – rather like honours doled out in the New Years' lists – that can also be conferred on the best wines, and act as a further endorsement of the wine's good pedigree. These are expressed in the local shorthand used by the country of origin. On French wine labels, the word 'Cru' has a significance. Cru actually means growth and is used in the sense of 'Grand Cru' – great growth; 'Cru Classe' – classed growth; 'Premier Cru' – first growth, and so on. Used in this way, 'cru' always indicates that the wine is in a superior class. 'Cru Bourgeois' indicates the wine is in a class behind. 'Mis en Bouteille' means 'put in bottle', and if the label confirms that this was done at the château or estate where the wine was grown, it again reflects additional quality. 'Villages' appearing on the label shows that the wine comes from a superior site in the wine-making area and suggests a better wine.

GERMANY

With characteristic attention to detail, German wines are all classified, pigeon-holed and ordered according to quality, making the labels as plain (to those who have cracked the code) as the numerical grading of eggs. In this northerly location, where sunshine can be rather meanly rationed out, the grapes' degree of ripeness is crucial to making good wine and it is therefore the sugar content of the freshly squeezed juice which determines the quality. This is scientifically monitored and given a score, and each score corresponds to a different quality status granted to each wine and declared on the label. Were no sweetening of the wines allowed at the bottom of the quality scale, the wines would quite simply get sweeter the higher up the scale they climbed. As it is, sugar is permitted to be added to the poorest 'musts', which makes them artificially 'medium' to taste and upsets the orderly graph.

At the bottom of the quality ladder is **Tafelwein**, Germany's 'Vin de Table'. Because Germany's climate is not suited to the mass-production of cheap wines, little 'Deutscher Tafelwein' is made. A lot of lookalikes abound on the wine shelves over here, however, and these are generally indifferent wines made elsewhere in the EEC, 'doctored' vaguely to taste like – and labelled in crude Gothic style to look like – the popular German-style wines.

Next up the scale comes **Landwein**, which is uncharacteristically dry or medium dry, and comes from (and is named after) a specified area. **Qualitatswein bestimmter Anbaugebeite (QbA)** – sorry about that – is quality wine from a designated area, and the example of this you are most likely to recognise is Liebfraumilch. Then starts the real ladder of quality (which intensifies in sweetness as it ascends) starting with **Qualitatswein mit Pradikat (QmP)**, meaning quality wine with a special distinction. The 'distinction' is a specified quality description and becomes more and more distinguished as you climb the scale: *Kabinett*, at the bottom end, is a light wine made from fully ripened grapes and is especially good with food. *Spatlese* is sweeter, made from late-picked grapes. *Auslese* is made from selected, very ripe bunches of grapes. *Beerenauslese* is made from individually selected over-ripe grapes and is very rich and sweet. *Eiswein* is made from grapes picked so late they are actually frozen when pressed, which concentrates the sugar – it is extremely rare. And *Trocken beerenauslese* is the sweetest of all – almost like honey – made from berries so ripe they look like raisins.

There are eleven separate German wine regions surrounding the two rivers, the Rhine and the Moselle. Each region is divided into districts known as 'Bereiches' (for example, Bereich Bernkastel), and may then be further divided into 'Grosslagen' (collections of vineyards) or 'Einzellagen' (single vineyards). As with the 'Appellation Contrôlée' in France, the more specific the declared origins of the wine, the better it is.

The best two regions as far as quality goes are the Rheingau, and the Moselle. Wines coming from the Rhine area are known here as hocks, and come in brown bottles, while Moselles come in green. The better German wines indicate on the label the individual grape varieties from which they are made, and the overall aristocrat is acknowledged to be Riesling.

ITALY

Table wine in any language usually indicates the most ordinary quality of wine, and in Italian the expression to look for on the label is **Vino da Tavola**. There's also a new title dreamed up: **Vini Tipici**, which describes a slightly more interesting sort of plonk with 'typical' characteristics of any given region, and this is equivalent to France's 'Vin de Pays'. **Denominazione di Origine Controllata (DOC)** is the official classification for quality wines. Some wine-makers, however, are a law unto themselves and it is sometimes not as reliable as it ought to be.

'DOC' is officially described as a 'definition of a tradition', stipulating what the wine ought to be like; but wines are not individually tested, so poor examples can (and do) slip through with this classification on the label. A more reliable indication of quality is offered by the 'DOCG' status, which is the same as 'DOC' with **e Garantita** ('and guaranteed') on the end. This guarantee is given only to certain wines – only five are so far eligible (Barbaresco, Barolo, Brunello di Montalcino, Chianti and Vino Nobile di Montepulciano) and to earn the title, the wines must pass stiff technical and tasting tests.

Additional 'handles' ascribed to Italian wines can be more reliable guides to real added quality than the classifications themselves. 'Classico', for example, shows that the wine has been produced in the heart of the region, in absolutely the best circumstances. 'Riserva' means that the wine has been matured for longer than is essential, and points to a smoother, mellower wine as a result. 'Superiore' indicates at least 1% more alcohol than the minimum required and generally goes hand in glove with better quality and more maturity. A Valpolicella boasting 'Amarone' on the label again shows that a higher degree of alcohol has been achieved, resulting in a drier, better wine.

SPAIN

Having only recently joined the EEC, Spain is in the process of reshaping the quality scale used for wines and radically altering some of the terms formerly used. Just to confuse matters, the description **Vino de Mesa** (meaning table wine) has hitherto been used for wines of slightly higher status (say, equivalent to 'VDQS') and **Vino de la Tierra** has been the term used for more ordinary wines. This looks likely to change.

Denominacion de Origen (DdeO) is the phrase used to qualify wines of higher quality, and 29 different regions and wines are now entitled to use this 'handle'. Traditionally, Spain has always been considered the home of good, honest plonk, but wine-making standards have improved so drastically across the whole country that you can now expect first rate quality from 'DdeO' wines.

On Spanish wine labels, all additional information about the wine's pedigree has to do with its age; as a general rule, the older the better (within reason), at least where reds are concerned. So 'Vino de Crianza' on the front or back label means the wine has spent at least 12 months in an oak cask and six in the bottle, before it is sold. 'Reserva' implies 12 months minimum in cask, with three more years in the bottle. 'Gran Reserva', the top category, shows a wine from an excellent harvest, with at least two years in cask and three in the bottle under its cork before it hits the shop shelves.

PORTUGAL

Vinho de Mesa is Portugal's table wine, and the humblest quality. No official category exists at present to identify the slightly better country wines, although their region may appear on the label. Plans are being worked on to introduce intermediate quality status. The top Portuguese wines come from officially demarcated and controlled regions marked on the label as **Região Demarcada.** Wines coming up to the region's minimum standards are granted an official number which appears either on a slip of paper placed over the cork, or, in the case of vinhos verdes, on the back label. The watchwords for 'pick-of-the-bunch' wines in Portugal are 'Reserva' and 'Garrafeira'.

Vintage

Grape variety

Region

Style (dry)

Volume in
centilitres

1986

70cl.

Sauvignon

BORDEAUX
SEC
APPELLATION BORDEAUX CONTRÔLÉE
Bottled in France by
MAISON DUPONT, DUPONTVILLE, BORDEAUX
PRODUCE OF FRANCE

11%vol

Country of origin
Where bottled

Quality status

Name and address of bottlers

Percentage of wine which is alcohol

EASTERN EUROPE, NORTH AND SOUTH AMERICA AND AUSTRALIA

In the newer wine-making regions of the world, which includes England, the individual grape varieties are the important guides on the label. Generally the poorer quality wines are made from blends of unspecified grapes and the better wines declare their grape varieties. Individual grape types are described in our A-Z.

THE BRANDS

While discussing indications of quality, brand-name wines should really also be considered as a separate category. Instead of being called after a specific place or region, or by a grape variety, they have been given product names which are then marketed and advertised, much as Coca-Cola is; and like Coca-Cola, brands can be relied upon for their entirely predictable taste.

Equivalent quality descriptions

Country	Description of ordinary table wine	Description of table wine with more character
France	Vin de Table	Vin de Pays
Germany	Deutscher Tafelwein	Landwein
Italy	Vino da Tavola	Vini Tipici
Spain	Vino de la Tierra	Vino de Mesa
Portugal	Vinho de Mesa	

Brands such as Nicolas, Corrida, Hirondelle, Blue Nun and Mateus Rosé, started out as cheap bulk wines in the days when the only alternative was expensive fine wines. The situation now is rather different. Their general price (which needs to support heavy advertising) is high compared to the wide choice of excellent wines now on offer in the high street. In fact, they are particularly expensive when you consider that the vast majority are merely of 'Vin de Table' status.

If you are looking for more variety in your wine drinking, it is perhaps best to avoid the homogenised brands: red Piat D'Or, for instance, is almost impossible to distinguish from white Piat D'Or in a blindfold test. In the past, the name Hirondelle was used for wines from thirteen different countries over a period of 11 years, but so exact is the formula for the finished drink, no-one ever seemed to notice. If you like the idea of complete uniformity in the taste of your wines (some would say dull repetition!) and you don't mind paying for it, then the brands are worth considering.

Quality wine	Top quality wine
VDQS (Vin Délimités de Qualité Supérieure)	Appellation Contrôlée
Qualitatswein bestimmter Anbaugebeite (QbA)	Qualitatswein mit Pradikat (QmP). described in ascending order as *Kabinett, Spatlese, Auslese, Beeranauslese, Eiswein* or *Trockenbeerenauslese*
Denominazione di Origine Controllata (DOC)	Denominazione di Origine Controllata e Garantita (DOCG)
	Denominacion de Origen (DdeO)
	Região Demarcada

Glossary

Increasingly, bottles have a back label to describe the characteristics of the wine inside. Below I have listed some of the most common words or phrases used by the industry when talking about wine. As you'll see, they are not nearly as difficult to understand as they appear.

Alcohol: Expressed as a percentage of the whole, wines range from 7°(7%) for a light white wine to 14°(14%) or more, for a gutsy, 'alcoholic' red.

Acidity: In moderation, a desirable component of most wines, off-setting the sweetness of the grape with a refreshing tang. When it is lacking, the wine tastes flat and dull.

Balanced: Describes a wine in which all the components and the range of taste sensations are balanced to complement each other, creating a harmonious whole.

Big: Used to describe heavy red wines that are generally high in alcohol, making them seem more substantial.

Body: The weight of a wine; light-bodied, medium or full-bodied. Goes with depth of flavour.

Bouquet: The aroma of a wine, best appreciated by putting your nose in the glass and having a good sniff.

Chambré: Room temperature, see page 161.

Crisp: Describes a wine with a refreshing, sharp tinge of acidity.

Clean: Pure tasting, with no 'off' flavours.

Complex: As the quality of the wine improves, so the scents and flavours gain more dimensions and greater depth. There is much more for the tongue to get around, and the mind to appreciate, so the wine is described as complex.

Corked: This does not mean there are bits of cork floating in the glass – nor most of the other unpleasantnesses that are frequently wrongly ascribed to this expression. A truly 'corked' wine smells rotten or musty because there is something wrong with the cork.

Dry: Describes a wine that contains little or no residual sugar: the opposite of sweet. A dry still wine may be described on the label as 'sec' (French); 'trocken' (German); 'secco' or 'asciutto' (Italian); 'seco' (Spanish and Portuguese). For sparkling wines, see page 158.

Fruity: A wine that reminds you of the fruit it is made from.

Fresh: Very slightly astringent and 'green' as in unripe fruit – but nonetheless a compliment.

Long: Refers to the length of time the flavour remains in the mouth once a sip has been swallowed. Better wines have a more lingering flavour.

Mature: A wine that is old enough for the flavours to have softened.

Medium/medium dry: Less dry than 'dry'. May be expressed on the label as 'demi-sec' (French); 'halbtrocken' (German); 'abboccato' (Italian); 'semi-seco' (Spanish); 'meio-seco' (Portuguese).

Medium/medium sweet: Less sweet than 'sweet'. May be expressed on the label as 'moelleux' (French); 'lieblich' (German); 'amabile' (Italian); 'semi-dulce' (Spanish); 'meio-doce' (Portuguese).

Mellow: Soft and well-rounded – no sharp, unharmonious flavours.

Nose: Like bouquet, means the scent of the wine.

Oak/oaky: Wines matured in oak casks assume some of the flavours of the wood, making the wine smell and taste slightly of vanilla.

Perlant: Very slightly fizzy.

Petillant: As perlant.

Ripe: A wine at its peak.

Round: A well-rounded wine, with no sharp edges to upset the harmony of the blend.

Sediment: Residual deposit left after fermentation, found in the bottle of some older red wines. It does not spoil the wine.

Soft: No harsh sensations in the flavour.

Spicey: The scent and flavour of spice in the wine.

Sweet: Describes a wine high in residual sugar: the opposite of dry. It may be expressed on the label as 'doux' (French); 'suss' (German); 'dolce' (Italian); 'dulce' (Spanish); 'doce' (Portuguese).

Tannin: A property contained in grape skins and stalks that makes the mouth feel dry and causes the cheeks to pucker when tasted in a young red wine destined to mature.

Tart: Sharp and tongue curling; too much acidity.

Woody: See oak.

Vintage: Simply refers to a wine made from grapes harvested in a single year (the year appearing on the label). Colloquially used to mean a fine old wine, but, in fact, young and inexpensive wines can be 'vintage' too.

Yeasty: It is a fault in a wine to be able to taste the yeast that is present during fermentation.

How much should you pay?

The answer to this question, of course, is another question: how long is a piece of string, or indeed, how deep is a wine lake? It's all relative. However, *Food and Drink* set about the stern task of exploring what you can buy for under £3, and there are, in fact, some very instructive guidelines; because the truth is that by spending as little as 30 pence more you can sometimes double the value (and quality) of the wine you are buying. It's also worth bearing in mind that the worst hangovers come from the cheapest wines; by spending that extra 30 pence you not only get a better taste but a significantly clearer head in the morning.

This is how the price works out. Over the page we have set out what costs a wine retailer incurs in getting a £1.99 bottle on the shelf. It's a modest wine he's bought in France to put under his own label: it's not a 'brand' nor is it a château-bottled vintage. He'll bring it back in bulk and bottle it in the UK. The cost of holding the stock will be 2 pence per bottle. Getting the wine to Britain plus the process of bottling set him back a further 11.25 pence. The label, cork and actual bottle cost a further 15.25 pence, and transportation in Britain along with storage and administration adds another 13 pence to the bill.

Now we approach 'le crunch'. How much is this canny fellow taking for himself? Well, if you add the cost of his advertising and sales activities to his profit you're still only looking at 36 pence. Far outweighing such paltry sums is the Excise Duty (at 68 pence) and the VAT (at 26 pence). It's the government, therefore, who demands the most generous slice of the cake.

But aren't we forgetting something: what's the value of the actual wine? As you can see, a miserly 27.5 pence. Now, imagine buying a bottle for £2.30 instead. Most of the above costs – bottling, transportation, advertising and duty – stay the same. The VAT rises, but only marginally. So by paying a mere 31 pence more you have bought a wine of double the value. The chances are that you will have doubled the quality, too. It's something to bear in mind as you look along the shelves.

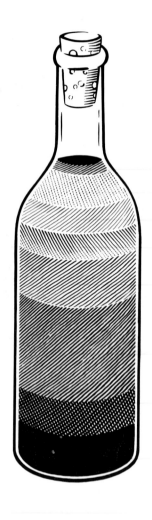

stock costs 2p

transport and bottling 11.25p

label, bottle, etc. 15.25p

UK transport, storage, admin 13p

profit, sales, advertising 36p

excise duty 68p

VAT 26p

value of wine 27.5p

total price: £1.99p

A-Z OF WINES

Since you can't ask to taste wines in supermarkets and off-licences, we have prepared an A-Z of the most familiar names on the wine shelves. In each case we try to give an indication of what sort of wine it is lurking behind the label. True to our declared intention, many of the wines below can be found for less than £3 a bottle. That, however, is not to say they are *always* less than £3 a bottle .... .

A

Alsace: Wine-making region in eastern France near the Rhine, responsible for making delicious dry white wines. Uniquely for France, most of the wines are named after grape varieties. Riesling is considered the best; a streamlined and delicately scented wine. Gewurztraminer (and to a lesser extent, Muscat) are both pungent, spicy wines. Alsace wines come in unusually tall green bottles and are consistently good: a reliable and yet unusual choice when eating out.

Anjou Rosé: Slightly sweet pink wine made both sides of the Loire River in France. Not generally of the highest quality, but fine for hot summer day drinking, taken straight from the fridge. It is best drunk as young as possible. Slightly better Anjou Rosés are made from the Cabernet Franc grape, and will say Cabernet on the label. Anjou Red and White are available too – both light in style.

Asti Spumante: Sweet, heady, sparkling wine from northern Italy, made from the highly aromatic Muscat grape. Must be drunk very young (best bought from a shop with a rapid turnover) and very cold. Can be offered on its own or with puddings and sweets, or of course – classically – with wedding cake.

B

Bardolino: A very light, though fruity red wine from the Verona district of Italy. It is hardly darker than deep rosé in colour and can be served either chilled or at room temperature.

Barolo: Italy's best red wine from the cooler, northerly district of Piedmont. A very 'big', full-bodied red wine which takes time to mature, so should not be drunk too young (seven or eight years old is a good age). It spends time ageing in oak barrels before being bottled. Serve at room temperature and take care pouring the wine when you get near the end of the bottle, because it may have 'thrown a sediment'. This does no harm to the wine, but looks unpleasant in the glass.

Beaujolais: Highly publicised red wine brought over to England in November as Beaujolais Nouveau, when it is only a few weeks old. Made in Beaujolais, the southern-most area of the Burgundy region, from the Gamay grape, it is characteristically purple and fresh, well suited to being drunk very young, when it should be chilled. Beaujolais Nouveau is usually finished by Easter, when it is replaced by ordinary Beaujolais, which should ideally never be drunk more than a year old. Beaujolais Villages is of a slightly superior quality, and can still be enjoyed a couple of years after the harvest. The finest Beaujolais are named after individual villages, or vineyard slopes, of which there are nine: Brouilly, Côte de Brouilly, Chénas, Chiroubles, Fleurie, Juliénas, Morgon, Moulin-à-Vent and St-Amour. Fleurie is one of the most popular, and lives up to its name as a very flowery wine, best drunk when it is two or three years old.

Bergerac: Wine region east of Bordeaux in France, making red wines similar to light clarets and variable whites, using the Sauvignon and Sémillon white Bordeaux grapes. Château Jaubertie is the name of an exceptional range of Bergerac wines made by an Englishman. The best sweet wines of the area are called Monbazillacs (see below), and are a good, inexpensive alternative to the fabulously expensive sweet Sauternes of Bordeaux.

Bernkastel: Famous town on the Moselle river, giving its name to quantities of fairly typical Moselle wines. Most are made from the Muller Thurgau grape and are fresh and crisp when very young. Those indicating they are made from Riesling grapes will generally be better.

Black Tower: A popular brand of Liebfraumilch (see below).

Blanc de Blancs: White wine made only from white grapes (hence 'white of whites'). Characteristically lighter in style than those white wines (particularly champagnes) which include some red grapes in their blend.

Blue Nun: One of the first famous brands of wine, which is now the best known wine in this country. It is a Liebfraumilch (see below) and as such is rather expensive.

Bordeaux: The classic red wine-producing region of France, home of all clarets (see below), on the outskirts of the town of Bordeaux on the West coast. The well-known wines, named after individual estates and châteaux, are largely very rich and rare. (They're only *for* the very rich too – tragically, often regarded as more of an investment than a drink these days.) Ordinary table wines, both red and white, do come out of this area as well, though, and you may see these labelled simply as

Bordeaux. The reds may be labelled Claret, and should not be too highly priced. These are good with red meat dishes, and should be opened a couple of hours before they are served. The best and most expensive white wines from the region are the lusciously sweet dessert wines, classically from Sauternes. The dry whites have shown a dramatic improvement recently and can now be quite a good buy (an example would be Entre-Deux-Mers), but they've never really been in the same league as the reds or sweet whites; this of course makes them more affordable.

Box: Wine boxes containing three or so litres of wine are the best way to buy wine for occasional drinkers who only want to pour the odd glass, being designed to keep the wine fresh for up to three months once opened. They do have their shortcomings, however. The technology of the collapsible, impervious bag and one-way-valve tap is expensive, so boxes are never a cheap way to buy wine, and if you intend to drink more than a few glasses at one time, you should really go for an ordinary bottle instead. For parties, regular-sized bottles usually work out as the cheapest buy.

British Wine: The only thing British about British wine is the water added to the grape concentrate, which is imported from abroad to be reconstituted and fermented over here. British wine is not 'real' wine at all, it's more like wine you make yourself from a kit. It used to enjoy a preferential tax rate, and so be very cheap, but this privilege no longer exists. Not to be confused with English Wine (see below).

Bulls' Blood: Northern Hungarian red wine from near Eger, named after an ancient legend. Supposedly, the men of Eger were downing the local wine before battle, and because they proved to be so brave and strong, the enemy thought they had been drinking bulls' blood instead. Hence the name, which is not exactly a brand – more the description of a quality wine from a particular area. Medium in weight and surprisingly light in alcohol.

Burgundy: One of the classic wine regions of France, famous for both its red and white wines. All wine entitled to call itself Burgundy or Bourgogne must be made from specified superior grape types (Pinot Noir for red and Chardonnay for white are the classics) and is above average in quality, though yields are small. Beaujolais (see above) is part of the Burgundy area, giving its name to a very individual type of red wine.

C

Cabernet Franc: Second cousin to the famous Cabernet Sauvignon red grape (see below), used as a secondary grape in making claret in Bordeaux, and for making the reds and better rosés of the Loire. In South America it is grown alongside the Cabernet Sauvignon and is likely to be included in any wine simply called Cabernet. A characteristic of this grape is an aroma of raspberries.

Cabernet Sauvignon: The most famous red grape variety, successfully cultivated around the world. In Bordeaux, it is the main grape behind the great clarets, slow-maturing and hard when young, but mellowing deliciously with age. New wine-making techniques mean it can now be used for quick-maturing, rich, fruity young wines, too. It always makes a good wine, wherever it is grown: in hotter areas, the fruitiness it produces is intensified, and you can get a veritable fruit-salad of a wine from it. Its most typical association is blackcurrants, particularly on the bouquet.

Canned wine: A bit of a gimmick really, unless you go on a lot of hikes and picnics. Although a comparatively expensive pack for wine (especially since they all come in small sizes), cans are good, indestructable containers and being coated with plastic inside, leave no metallic taste in the wine.

Carafe: Carafe-shaped wine containers introduced into this country by the Californians, make attractive 'alternative' wine bottles, especially for dinner parties. They do, however, bump up the cost of the wine a bit. In a restaurant, if you order the 'carafe' wine, make sure you know how much you will be getting for your money, a quarter, half or a full litre, and that the size is adequately reflected in the price.

Cava: Spain's best sparkling wines use the name 'Cava' on the label to distinguish themselves from lesser sparklers and are made in the same painstaking method as champagne. They are generally softer and less astringent than real champagne, and although not quite in the same class, offer good value for money as party wines or for private celebrations.

Chablis: Best known of all the great white Burgundies made from the Chardonnay grape, Chablis has suffered as a result of its popularity. Many of the most common supermarket and off-licence Chablis are frankly disappointing for the price. Better examples are described on the label as 'Premier Cru', and the best and, of course, most expensive, as 'Grand Cru'.

Champagne: Sparkling wine may only be called champagne if it is made from specific varieties of red and white grape, by a thoroughly labour-intensive method, and in a precisely defined area north-east of Paris. It is indisputedly the best sparkling wine in the world, although not all champagnes are equally good. The best, and generally the most expensive, are vintage champagnes, declaring the year when the wine was made on the bottle. Of the 'non vintage' champagnes without a date on the label, the ones with famous names are generally better than the rest. See also **Sparkling Wines**.

Chardonnay: Perhaps the greatest white grape variety, cultivated throughout the world. In its traditional home, Burgundy, it can produce fantastically complex wines which balance a rich 'buttery' taste with a refreshing sting of acidity. The light-style 'blanc de blancs' champagnes are made exclusively from the Chardonnay grape. In hotter areas, such as California and Australia, it produces 'bigger', fuller wines with more alcohol, sometimes so rich they almost seem sweet. Reasonably-priced Chardonnays are made in Bulgaria, Italy, untypical areas of France and New Zealand.

Châteauneuf-du-Pape: A hearty, full-bodied red wine from the Rhône valley in France, with a high content of alcohol. Unusually, it is made from a blend of about 12 different grape varieties. It is at its best between five and ten years old and is a good match for substantial red meat and game dishes and casseroles.

Chenin Blanc: This grape variety's home is in the Loire, where it produces Anjou Blanc, Saumur (still and sparkling) and Vouvray (dry, medium and sweet, still and sparkling): these wines all have a faintly honeyed smell and are quite light and fresh. In California it makes rather bland, medium wines and in South Africa it is known as Steen and produces a slightly fizzy, *petillant* wine.

Chianti: The standard of Chianti recently became so unreliable (as huge quantities were being produced to satisfy escalating demand around the world) that in 1984 the Italian government stepped in and declared that all Chianti must either raise its standards to qualify for the DOCG title (see page 135) or give up its right to the name altogether. All Chiantis made after 1984 are generally much improved as a result. Wines from the Chianti district not up to scratch must now be called by another name, for example Rosso di Toscana. As a rule, the better examples of Chianti come in ordinary bottles – the wicker flasks, although they once had their use in stabilising irregular bottle shapes, are now an expensive and unnecessary gimmick.

Claret: Traditional English name coined for the red wines of Bordeaux. Although Claret is used conversationally for the finest red Bordeaux (see above), its appearance on a label in fact indicates a lesser wine – a basic Appellation Bordeaux Contrôllée.

Concorde: British wine made from grape concentrate imported from abroad, made slightly sparkling with injected gas.

Corbières: Fairly alcoholic, full-bodied red wine from the Languedoc and Roussillon areas of southern France.

Corrida: Brand name of a range of Spanish wines that has recently smartened up its image. The full red is a beefy wine, needing to 'breathe' for an hour or two before it is tackled (see page 162). The medium dry is a bit on the sweet side, but pleasantly clean and fresh.

Côtes du Rhône: General name for the 30-million-plus gallons of ordinary wine produced a year in the 120 mile stretch of the Rhône Valley. In general, the wines are light and unexceptional; a slightly spicy earthiness is sometimes discernible and quality is very variable. As usual, more reliability is offered when either a village name is included on the label, or simply the word 'Villages'.

D

Dão: Best known (quality) red wine area of Portugal, producing strong, dry, full-bodied wines that acquire a velvetiness from storage in oak barrels. Good, mature red Dãos are generally moderately priced and well worth trying. The whites can be enjoyable, too, and are characteristically dry and 'flinty' tasting.

Don Cortez: The brand name for a range of Spanish wines that have recently undergone a total facelift. Modern wine-making techniques introduced into their rustic regions of origin have improved the wines immeasurably. They are now much lighter and fresher than formerly, and well priced.

E

English Wine: England is surprisingly well suited to the growing of wine-making grapes and the making of white wines (we're not so good with red). Because wine has been made commercially here for only a short time, the EEC only allows it to be described as 'Table Wine' at present, but the wines produced are in fact quality wines, all 'estate grown' and 'estate bottled' (i.e. not mass-produced) which accounts for their slightly high prices.

Entre-deux-Mers: Dry, Sauvignon-based white wine from the area between the rivers Garonne and Dordogne (the two 'mers' or seas) of Bordeaux which is classically teamed with seafood.

F

Fleurie: Superior Beaujolais from an individual village, generally flowery in style. (See Beaujolais.)

Frascati: Almost colourless white wine made now in the suburbs of the ever-expanding city of Rome. Second in fame only to Soave, and consequently being 'stretched' to meet increasing worldwide demand: quality is consequently rather erratic.

G

Gamay: The red grape variety behind all Beaujolais, unique in its ability to make super-light, fruity, young red wines almost more like white wines in style. It has now been introduced to other areas in France such as the Ardeche, the Auvergne and the Loire, and to Eastern Europe, where it makes similarly styled wines called simply Gamay. In California, the true Gamay goes to make wines called Napa Gamay and a rather sweet, inferior wine is called Gamay Beaujolais.

Gewürztraminer: Gewürz means spicy, and wines made from this assertive grape type, which may be either dry or medium dry, are all unusually spicy to taste (almost sweet-and-sour) and have a pungent bouquet reminiscent of tropical fruit. The traditional home of Gewürztraminer wines is Alsace in France, and they are also now made in Austria, Australia, California, Italy and Yugoslavia. They may also be labelled simply as Traminer.

Graves: This is a huge area of the Bordeaux region producing a range of red and white wines of all qualities (including the sweet whites, Barsac and Sauternes: for the latter, see below). If you see the name 'Graves' actually on the label of a bottle, however, the wine will be of a fairly ordinary quality. As a general rule, dry whites from the region are in green bottles and sweet whites are in clear bottles.

H

Hermitage/Crozes-Hermitage: Hermitage, named after a hill, is the classic red wine of the northern Rhône, made from Syrah grapes. It is rich in style – quite like a Burgundy – and is very long lived. Crozes-Hermitage is the name given to the less noble wines from the surrounding area. Both names are also given to white wines, which again are quite rich and almost nutty in character.

Hirondelle: Brand name for a range of ordinary quality table wines. The red, white and rosé come from Italy, the sweet white from Cyprus and the Liebfraumilch from Germany. Wines with the Hirondelle label have come from all sorts of different locations in the past, demonstrating that the important thing about a brand is not the wine itself but the name (see page 138).

Hock: Name reputedly given to the wines from the Rhine Valley in Germany by Queen Victoria. Now used on labels simply to describe an ordinary blend of table wine from any of the regions of the Rhine.

L

Lambrusco: Slightly fizzy, generally sweet red or white wine from Italy. Quality varies enormously and there are a few simple pointers as to what's what. The red styles are the most typical and the best: look for 'Denominacione di Origine Controllata' on the label, and for a cork rather than a screw cap. There are four districts and DOC Lambruscos will all proclaim which one they come from. The best is Sorbara and second best is Grasparossa di Castelvetro. 'Amabile' on the label indicates a sweet style, and more unusually, 'Secco', dry. The better Lambruscos acquire their sparkle naturally during fermentation and will probably declare 'Fermentazione Naturale' on the label to prove it. Less enjoyable versions are simply injected with CO_2, as is lemonade. Both red and white Lambruscos should be served well chilled and are best as aperitifs on their own, rather than with food.

Laski Riesling: Laski, Olacz, Welsch Rieslings and Riesling Italico are all poor relations of the highly-refined Riesling grape, producing less distinguished wines; aromatic, pungently fruity and slightly sweet. Their main shortcoming is that they lack a bite of fresh acidity and can be a little 'flabby' as a result. Well chilled, they are nonetheless easy and appealing wines to drink. They mainly come from Eastern European countries and from Italy.

Liebfraumilch: The most popular German wine in Britain, Liebfraumilch is produced especially for the British market (there is none sold in Germany). It ranks as a QbA, the lowest status for quality German wines, and must come from specific regions and be made from specified grape types. The cheapest examples still manage to be rather poor though, so it is well worth paying a few more pence for a better wine. Crown of Crowns is a good name to go for.

Lutomer: Brand name for a Laski Riesling wine from Yugoslavia.

M

Mâcon: The sub-region of Burgundy responsible for producing the least expensive reds and whites of the area (which, bearing in mind the astronomical price of some Burgundies, isn't *that* cheap). The whites, made from the Chardonnay grape, are the more remarkable and offer an affordable suggestion of the greatest white wines in the world.

Mateus Rosé: Pink, slightly sparkling brand from Portugal. Not of exceptional quality, but as with all brands, consistent in taste and quality.

Médoc: Wines labelled simply Médoc (almost all red) are the lesser mortals of perhaps the greatest wine-making area in the world; the most prestigious portion of Bordeaux.

Minervois: VDQS red wine from the South of France, with lots of class and character. Fragrant and full-bodied; generally a very good buy.

Monbazillac: Luscious, sweet white wine from the Bergerac region south of Bordeaux (see page 147). The young versions make surprisingly good aperitifs, and the more mature, rich, voluptuous dessert wines.

Moscato Spumante: Light, sparkling wine, young and sweet, made from the pungent Muscat grapes. A cheaper alternative to Asti Spumante (see above).

Mosel/Moselle: German river lending its name to a whole family of white wines made along its banks. Those simply called Moselle on the label are the most basic in quality – light, greenish (and bottled in green bottles) medium-dry white wines.

Mouton Cadet: Red and white Bordeaux wines boasting the famous Mouton name and coming from the Mouton-Rothschild stable. Rather expensive for what they are – particularly on restaurant wine lists – but of reliable quality, the reds being well enough made to mature gracefully into better wines, if you are prepared to store them for a year or two.

Muscadet: Light, dry white wine made in the Loire Valley from the grape of the same name. Ordinary Muscadet is rather over-produced, and can lack guts and personality, being rather wishy-washy as a result. Better versions come from the area surrounding two tributories of the Loire, labelled as Muscadet de Sèvre-et-Maine. Another sign of quality to look for is Sur Lie, meaning the wine has remained in contact for a while with the sediment left after fermentation, which results in a more robust, fruity, characterful wine. All Muscadets should be drunk young – a year or two after the vintage date, if there is one on the label.

Muscat: Muscatel-like grape, responsible for making pungent, spicy, fruity wines: both dry, such as the Muscat wines from Alsace, and sweet, such as those made in Australia and Portugal.

Muscat de Beaumes-de-Venise: A lightly fortified (with brandy) dessert wine from the Rhône Valley, currently enjoying a fashionable phase.

N

Navarra: Wine-making region in northern Spain bordering the Pyrenees renowned for good rosados (rosés). The fruity reds are becoming increasingly light in style, and those other than 'reservas' should be drunk young. In common with many Spanish wines, they are reliable and well-priced.

Nicolas: One of the pioneer branded French wines – incidentally, highly respected in France.

Nierstein: A major Bereich of the German Rhineland, responsible for making soft, light white wines, frequently too cheap for their own good. 'Gutes Domtal' on the label indicates the wine comes from a huge 'grosslage' (collection of vineyards) within the Nierstein catchment, but does not mean the wine is necessarily of any better quality. 'Niersteiner' on the label simply means a wine from the Nierstein area.

Nouveau: New wine, sold only weeks after the grapes are harvested. In general, wine made in the autumn only appears on the wine shelves in the following spring, at the earliest. Nouveau appears any time from late October, and is sold only until the the new year. Beaujolais nouveau was the classic, but now new wines from all over the world are becoming available, both reds and whites. (Because the seasons are different, southern hemisphere nouveaux first arrive on the shelves in spring.) The whites can be a bit too astringent and raw, but the reds can have a delicious fresh fruitiness to them, and are best drunk chilled.

O

Olacz Riesling: See Laski Riesling.
Orvieto: Light, fresh Italian white wine, traditionally sweet (described as 'Abboccato' or 'Amabile' on the label) with an appealing hint of almond; the modern, dry version (secco) is often rather dull and characterless.

P

Paul Masson: Name behind the original carafes of wine from California. These not only introduced an attractive new style of wine container into this country but also an attractive new style of wine, being obviously fruity and marginally sweet. As well as the carafes, there is now a well-priced range of higher quality Paul Masson Californian wines in ordinary bottles made from individual grape varieties.
Perlwein: Slightly fizzy (usually rather poor quality) white wine from Germany found in ordinary 'still' wine bottles. The gentle bubbles are pretty and refreshing, but short-lived.
Le Piat d'Or: Top-selling brand of French table wines; both the red and white are slightly sweet and virtually indistinguishable. Their success is attributable more to clever packaging and advertising than to the taste and quality of the wine (which is actually rather over-priced for what it is).
Piesport: Best-known village name on the Moselle, responsible for making some delicious (though expensive) Riesling wines, especially from the individual vineyard called Goldtropfchen. Michelsberg is the name of a collection of vineyards responsible for producing considerably lower quality wines which vary from dull to average.
Pinot Noir: Grape behind all the great red Burgundies, capable of making soft, velvety wines. Young Pinot Noir wines are reminiscent of raspberries; older versions seem almost high, like well-hung game. Unlike Cabernet Sauvignon, Pinot Noir vines do not travel well, and examples from hotter locations such as Australia and California can be too intense and alcoholic, making them rather 'full blown'. Spain and Italy produce some good Pinot Noirs (Italy's can be called Pinot Nero, or Blauburgunder in the Tyrol).

R

Retsina: A Greek wine, flavoured with wood resin. An acquired taste, delicious with Greek food and barbecues.

Riesling: Grape variety also known as Rhine Riesling or Johannisberg Riesling, used in most of Germany's top quality wines. It produces a delicate wine with a flowery fragrance: light in body, high in refreshing acidity and distinctly fruity. It is a much more streamlined variety than the Laski and Olacz Rieslings of Eastern Europe (see page 153).

Rioja (pronounced riocca): Top wine-producing area of Spain located in the north, just south of Basque country. Red Riojas are generally aged in oak casks for a time, giving the wine a mellowness and a noticeable vanilla flavour. Traditionally, Riojas are matured for a long time before being sold – within reason, 'the older the better' is a good rule of thumb. White Riojas also used to be aged in wood and kept to mature, resulting in lovely rich, golden, full-bodied wines such as Marques de Murrietta. The new style (discernible by either a recent date, or no date at all on the label) are much lighter in body and more run of the mill.

Rocamar: Another brand of often indifferent Spanish wine.

S

Sancerre: Tartly fresh white wines from the Loire made from the distinctive Sauvignon grape. Clean and refreshing, they are popular and tend to be quite expensive; cheaper alternatives are labelled Sauvignon de Touraine. Small quantities of light-style red Sancerres can be found too.

Sansovino: Reliable range of branded Italian wines, the Bianco (white) being fairly medium-sweet, the Bianco Secco, medium-dry and the Vino Rosso, ordinarily red.

Saumur: Major wine-producing area on the south bank of the river Loire, responsible for making still white wines from the Chenin Blanc grape, rosés and reds from the Cabernet Franc and most importantly, good-quality, sparkling white wines made by the traditional champagne method.

Sauternes: With Barsac, an adjoining wine-making area in Bordeaux, Sauternes is responsible for making the richest, fattest, most concentrated and most expensive sweet white wines in the world. Unique conditions in the area concentrate the sugar in the grapes, but only in exceptional years. Sweet white wines are still produced when the conditions are *not* perfect, but although still expensive, they are not outstanding. A cheaper alternative such as a Monbazillac or a sweet Muscat is a better buy among dessert wines.

Sauvignon: White grape type producing very dry wines with a pungent, strong character. Sancerre and Pouilly Fumé wines from the Loire are made from the Sauvignon grape, as are many dry white Bordeaux. Other areas use the grape – and say so on the label – and if they're drunk young these wines are reliably fresh and crisp. In sunnier areas such as Yugoslavia, the wines are less astringent and have more of an aroma of freshly mown grass. Sauvignon is sometimes called Fumé Blanc in California.

Sekt: Germany's name for sparkling wine, even though most Sekt is not German. The name may be used for wines bought anywhere in the EEC (often taken from the so-called wine lake of surplus poor-quality wine) but they are transported to Germany to be made sparkling. As from September 1986, all sparkling wine labelled German Sekt or Deutscher Sekt must be 100% German. Deutscher Sekt bestimmer Anbaugebiete (bA) has to come from a specified wine region and be made from specific grape varieties, and it is of better quality as a result. Much ordinary Sekt is pretty basic and raw. Of the Deutscher Sekts, Deinhard's Cuvée Lila made from the Riesling grape is highly recommended.

Soave: Most famous white wine from Italy; light, dry and unlikely to cause offence. Over-popularity has made it rather an industrial product and the worst examples are neutral to the point of being unacceptably bland. A reliable name to look for is Bolla.

Sparkling Wines: Recent legislation by the EEC now controls the description that appears on the label of the sweetness and dryness of sparkling wines and champagne:

Extra brut (French) or *extra herb* (German) – a wine with virtually no residual sugar. The dryest wines in the world.

Brut (French) or *herb* (German) – a wine that is marginally less dry. Bone dry. May also be called *extra dry* or *extra trocken* (German).

Sec (French); *trocken* (German); *secco* or *ascuito* (Italian); *seco* (Spanish and Portuguese): a dry wine.

Demi-sec (French); *halbtrocken* (German); *abboccato* (Italian); *semi-seco* (Spanish); *meio-seco* (Portuguese): a medium dry wine.

Doux (French); *mild* (German); *dolce* (Italian); *dulce* (Spanish); *doce* (Portuguese): a sweet wine.

Syrah: One of the mainstay black grapes of red Rhône wines, suited to making dark, chewy, tannic wines with a slightly smoky taste and terrific depth. Frequently used to 'beef up' wines from the South of France, it now also appears on labels in its own right, being the grape behind some pretty hefty, characterful wines. In Australia it is known as the Shiraz, and makes pungently spicy red wines.

T

Tafelwein: German for table wine. 'Tafelwein' on the label points to one of two things: either the wine is a genuine Deutscher Tafelwein made in Germany (and in this case look for the word 'Deutscher' on the label) or a crafty lookalike coming from the ubiquitous European wine lake of cheap and undistinguished wine. The latter will say somewhere on the label 'wine from different countries of the European Community' and though made to look (and taste) like a German wine is actually nothing of the sort. Frequently EEC blends are very cheap, which is perhaps one redeeming feature.

Tavel Rosé: High-quality dry, full-bodied, unusually alcoholic rosé from the Rhône valley, well matched with quite substantial meals.

V

Valpolicella: Very light red wine from Italy, which, like Beaujolais, should be drunk young and can be chilled. In league with other popular Italian wines, Valpolicella is over-produced, and at the bottom end of the range can be rather thin and uninteresting, so it is worth paying a bit more for a better wine from a respectable producer. Also, look for marks of higher quality – 'Classico' and 'Superiore' on the label. A dry, heavier version is labelled 'Amarone'.

Verdicchio (pronounced with a hard c): One of Italy's most popular white wines (along with Frascati, Orvieto and Soave), sometimes found in distinctive amphora-shaped bottles. Generally dry, the best come from either the Classico area of Castelli di Jesi or from Mattelica.

Veuve du Vernay: Best-selling brand of sparkling wine in the UK. Nevertheless of rather ordinary quality, made by a bulk process known as 'Cuve Close' or 'Charmat'. Consistent, but never great; as a change try a Saumur or a Cava, which have rather more finesse and style.

Vinho Verde: Meaning 'green wine', this is Portugal's most popular white wine; the 'green' merely refers to the fact that it is drunk very young. The most commercial types are slightly sweet, though better quality examples such as Quinta da Aveleda and Gazela are now following the trend, being slightly drier. They are all marginally sparkling, which makes them quite festive; delicious to drink well-chilled in summer. Perfect wine for outdoors.

Vouvray: Slightly sweet white wine from north of the Loire river. The sparkling version is made in the classic champagne method.

Z

Zinfandel: Californian grape variety responsible for making some robust, inky-dark red wines with considerable depth of flavour. On Victoria Wine's scale, they would definitely be called 'big' and 'firm'. Sometimes the grape is made into 'white' wine, which actually turns out to be rather meaty and pink.

SERVING WINE: A FEW SIMPLE RULES

No-one makes much fuss about how to serve beer, beyond whether you like a mug with a handle or a straight-sided glass, so why all the fuss and palava over wine? Much of the performance is certainly quite unnecessary and serves little purpose beyond creating a sense of occasion (which in itself isn't such a bad thing, admittedly, especially if you are entertaining or eating out in a restaurant). Observing some of the simpler rituals, however, such as getting the temperature right, can actually increase your enjoyment of any bottle of wine, no matter how cheap. Unlike virtually all beers you can drink at home, wine is still very much 'alive' and is pretty susceptible to the treatment you give it. So it is worth following a few rules.

SERVING TEMPERATURES

Centuries ago, when wine was really only served in the grandest of houses, it was discovered that white and rosé wines tasted at their freshest and best when drunk straight from the cellar (i.e. cold), while reds (also stored in chilly cellars) needed to warm up to the temperature of the room before they would 'open up' and allow the drinker to appreciate all their potential aromas and flavours. Few cellars were as cold as the modern fridge, however, and certainly no room was as warm as our centrally-heated (or at least insulated) homes today. So the danger now is that we thoroughly overdo the instructions to 'chill' or 'serve at room temperature', often either completely 'numbing' or totally 'cooking' the wine. White, rosé and sparkling wines can become completely subdued and characterless if they are tasted too cold. An hour or two in the door of the fridge is usually enough, or, for more rapid chilling, 10 minutes immersed up to the neck of the bottle in cold water and ice. (In dire emergencies the freezer can be used very briefly – certainly no more than 10 minutes. This is better than drinking the wine warm, but will kill some of the subtleties of better wines.)

When 'room temperature' was the phrase coined for the ideal serving temperature for red and dark fortified wines, houses were much cooler than they are now. A red wine that has been waiting to be opened anywhere other than a cellar, the garage in winter or a fridge will be quite warm enough to serve. Should a bottle of red wine be considered too cold, it should never be heated artificially by a fire, stove or radiator: any drastic temperature change would impair the flavour. The ideal is to keep the bottle in the room with you for a couple of hours until it has warmed up, but if you cannot wait, open the bottle up and pour the wine into glasses and you can bring it to life quite quickly by cupping the glass in your hand.

WHEN TO OPEN THE BOTTLE

All white wines can be opened when you are ready for them and poured right away, but red wines may be put through all kinds of hoops before they are served. In a restaurant, a bottle of red may be opened ahead of time and left on the side to allow it to breathe; it may be presented to you reclining in a wicker basket, or if you are being given the full works, it can be transferred into a crystal decanter. But how much of all this fuss and bother is entirely necessary?

Well, wicker baskets were originally intended to keep the wine unclouded by sediment when taken straight from the rack. Since few wines now have sediment, however, and wine waiters invariably rotate and shake the bottle when removing the cork anyway, they now serve little purpose and are usually merely decorative.

In my opinion, all but the oldest red wines do actually improve a bit and become more overt when exposed to the air for a while before you take your first sip. Removing the cork from the bottle ahead of time will have a very marginal effect on the wine – since the area exposed to the air is very small, so too will be the effect. If, however, you pour out a glass or two, more air can get at the wine, and you will find that you can notice a difference between a sip taken from a freshly opened bottle and one taken half an hour later from either bottle or glass.

Pouring the wine into a different container, or 'decanting' it as this practice is known, was originally intended to separate the clean wine from any sediment remaining in the bottom of the bottle. Few of the types of wines most of us drink today actually throw any sediment in the bottle, so this purpose is now largely defunct. There is no better way to aerate a red wine, however, than to pour it out of the bottle, through the air into another container – the ideal being a decanter or carafe. The added advantage of decanting wine is that it looks so elegant, particularly if you are entertaining.

HOW LONG WILL IT KEEP?

Once opened and exposed to the air, wine gradually starts to go off. It is susceptible to all sorts of anti-social elements in the air, and will go way past its best within the space of 24 hours. You can marginally extend the life of opened white wines by recorking them and returning them to the fridge, and reds will hang on to their freshness for a little longer if poured into a spotlessly clean half bottle and recorked. The rescue operation will have a limited effect though: even if you only intend to keep the wine for cooking, it will turn too sour to enhance any dish within four to five days. The best solution, therefore, is either to use it up quickly, or, for occasional drinkers, to rely on wine boxes instead (especially designed to keep the wine fresh once opened).

STORING WINE

In the past, wines used to take a long time to mature before they were ready to drink. Instead of keeping them until they reached their prime, wine merchants would sell their wines too young to drink and customers were expected to mature them at home themselves. Now, by contrast, most wines are ready to drink straight from the wine shop shelves and many (especially the brand-names and the very cheapest wines) are best drunk straight away and not kept at all. The wine brands and ordinary table wines actually have a very limited life – most should be consumed within six months of first appearing in the shop. There is even talk of such wines being given 'sell by' dates.

But not all wines need to be polished off as soon as you get them home. Among the better quality wines, all reds except the very lightest styles and cheap champagnes, for example, actually improve with time (within reason, of course – they don't go on getting better for ever). And if you store them at home you will actually be doing the wines – and yourselves – a favour. Because wine is alive, the conditions for storage must be kind: direct heat or sunlight on the bottle is a bad thing and so is a temperature which often varies. Bottles are best kept in a cool cupboard or corner, away from too much direct light, and stored on their sides. This *is* essential, since if the cork is allowed to dry out it becomes loose, letting in the air and spoiling the wine.

CORKSCREWS

New fangled corkscrews are designed every year to attract Christmas shoppers and many of them are too gimmicky to do a good job. Essentially, you need an 'open' spiral or helix (with space in the middle of the spiral), not a screw with a solid shaft. The latter can tear the cork and fail to remove it, or can push particles of the cork down into the wine. Cork in the glass does no harm, but looks unpleasant and needs to be fished out. Sometimes the whole cork starts to slide down into the bottle as you try to insert the corkscrew: in this instance there is little you can do except push it very gently down into the bottle and then either pour each glass very carefully, or decant the whole bottle of wine into another container. The stem of a teaspoon lowered into the neck of the bottle will prevent the cork blocking the top of the bottle as you pour the first glass. There is also a type of corkscrew around that can rescue a damaged cork, and this has two flat shafts that you can ease down the side of the cork, and gradually rock the cork out. As corkscrews go, The Screwpull is one of the best (although admittedly over-priced) having not only an ideal screw with a good helix, but also a cleverly designed mechanism to assist the withdrawal of the cork.

OPENING SPARKLING WINES

Contrary to the popular image, a champagne cork does not have to blast off explosively leaving a dent in the ceiling. By observing a few simple rules you can ensure that all the sparkling wine ends up in the glass rather than all over the floor.

1 Before removing the metal foil, locate the wire twist and unwind it. Keeping your thumb on top of the cork (just in case the cork is in the mood to fly off), pull off the wire muzzle, the foil and finally the metal cap on top of the cork.

2 Still holding on to the cork, tilt the bottle to an angle of about 45° – if the bottle is inclined at an angle, when the cork is removed, the trapped CO_2 can escape without taking any wine with it.

3 Holding the cork firmly in one hand and the bottle in the other (still at 45°), twist the bottle gently until the cork begins to ease out. You should then hear a hiss as the air escapes. The cork can then be taken fully out, and the first glass poured. If you twist the cork instead of the bottle, you run the risk of breaking it off. If by chance this happens, you must be extremely careful, since the pressure inside a champagne bottle is equivalent to that in the tyres of a London bus. If you are very careful, you can apply a corkscrew to the remaining bit of cork – still keeping the bottle at an angle – and ease it out very gently.

If you observe these simple rules the cork will come out in your hand with a gentle pop, the sparkling wine will stay in the bottle and your skill will be admired by all and sundry.

GLASSES

There is an enormous range of glasses available in the shops for wine: many far too fussy and elaborate for the job, because the basic rule with wine glasses is: the simpler the better. The ideal wine glass is clear so you can appreciate the exact colour of the wine. Not only is this attractive but it can tell you a bit about the wine; as they get older, red wines begin to turn from purple to brown, and white wine from pale to gold.

A stem to hold the glass by is a necessary part of the design, to prevent the temperature of your hand from affecting the temperature of the wine. The bowl should be narrower at the brim than in the body, so that the aroma (or 'bouquet') can be trapped in the glass. You get the most out of the aroma if the wine glass is no more than half or two-thirds filled, because it builds up in the empty space in the glass.

It is certainly not necessary to own a full range of glasses. You can either use just one basic all-round shape, or in time collect various different designs and sizes for different types of wine.

INDEX

Entries in italics refer to wine

Alsace 28, 104, 146
Anjou Rosé 146
Apples
  Baked with Honey 78
  Basic Apple Chutney 97
  Cox 124
  Golden Delicious 124
Artichokes 64
Asti Spumanti 108, 131, 146
Auslese 108, 134
Avocado Milkshake 18

Bardolino 146
Barbaresco 135
Barolo 135, 146
Beaujolais 45, 104, 147
Beef 50, 51
  Anton Mosimann's Poached Fillet of 52
  Pot-roasted Silverside 53
Beerenauslese 134
Bergerac 147
Bernkastel 147
Black Tower 147
Blanc de Blancs 147
Blue Nun 139, 147
Bordeaux 147
Borscht 114
Bread 83-91
  brown 84
  Brown Soda 86
  wheatgerm 84
  White Soda 86
  wholemeal 84
Bread and Butter Pudding, Anton Mosimann's 91
Brownies, Chocolate 75
Brunello di Montalcino 135
Brussels Sprouts and Mushrooms with Mustard Seeds and Garlic 112
Bulls' Blood 148
Burgundy 148

Cabernet Franc 149
Cabernet Sauvignon 52, 149
Cake
  Chocolate, Instant 74

Marmalade 81
Cava 149
Celeriac, Purée of 66
Chablis 149
Champagne 150, 158, 165
Chardonnay 96, 130, 150
Châteauneuf-du-Pape 150
Cheddar and Anchovy Toast 89
Cheese 92-96
  Appleby Farmhouse Cheshire 95
  Beenleigh 96
  Bonchester 95
  Cumberland Farmhouse 95
  Llangoffan 95
  Neal's Yard Creameries 96
  Single Gloucester 96
  Three Shires 96
Cheese and Salami on Granary 88
Chenin Blanc 150
Chianti 135, 150
Chicken 33-47
  Chinese Chicken and Peppers 47
  Cockie Leekie Soup 47
  Dijon Pancakes 45
  Elastic Chicken, The 41
  Florentine 46
  and Lettuce Parcels 36
  Normandy Style 38
  Oriental 37
  Provençal 43
  Stock 39
  and Sweetcorn Soup 44
Chocolate
  Brownies 75
  Instant Chocolate Cake 74
  Orange Chocolate Mousse 77
  Truffles 108
Christmas Pudding, Low-Fat 106
Chutneys 97-98
Claret 52, 151
Cod Chowder, New England 31
Concorde 151
Corbières 91, 151
Corrida 139, 151
Côtes du Rhône 151

Croûtons, Garlic and Herb 89
Custard, Classic Baked 82

Dão 52, 151
Don Cortez 151

Eggs 10-11, 14, 15, 87
  quails' 10, 15
  Wholemeal Baps with Egg and Cress 87
Eiswein 134
English Wines 28
Entre-deux-Mers 152
Exotic Stir-Fry 65

Fleurie 104, 152
Frascati 152

Gamay 56, 152
Gewürztraminer 104, 152
Goose, Roast 104
Graves 152

Herring, Chopped, on Black Rye 87
Herrings in Oatmeal 25
Hunter's Loaf 88

Irish Stew, Myrtle Allen's 54

Lambrusco 153
Laski Riesling 153
Latkes 113
Liebfraumilch 131, 154
Lutomer 154

Mâcon 154
Madhur Jaffrey's Christmas Recipes 109-111
Mallard 101
Mateus Rosé 91, 139, 154
Médoc 154
Mince Pies, Low-Fat
Mincemeat 107

Minervois 91, 132-3, 154
Monbazillac 80, 154
Monkfish in Green
  Peppercorn Sauce 24
Monkfish Kebabs 23
Moscato Spumante 154
Mosel/Moselle 154
Mosimann, Anton 10, 52,
  68, 91, 94
Mousse, Orange Chocolate
  77
Mouton Cadet 154
Muscadet 155
*Muscadet de Beaumes-
  de-Venise* 80, 155

Nicolas 139

Oat Pancakes 80
Olacz Riesling 156
Onion Bhaji 16
Orange Almond Crunch
  76
Orange Chocolate Mousse
  77
Oranges in Caramel 76
Orvieto 156
Oysters, Baked 32

Pancakes 45, 79, 80
Paul Masson 156
Pear and Stilton Starter
  17
Perlwein 156
Pheasant .101, 103
Piat d'Or, Le 139, 156
Piesport 156
Pinot Noir 156
Pitta and Haloumi 90
Plantain, Fried 67
Pork 49, 50
Port 96

Potatoes
  Anton Mosimann's
    Potato Dish 68
  Crispy Roast 68
  Fried with Fennel
    Seeds 109
  Latkes 113
  Pommes de Terre
    Dauphinoise 69
Prawns
  Louisiana 27
  Sweet-and-Sour 26
Pumpkin Pie 73
Pumpkin Soup (Fondo del
  Sol) 12

Quinn, Michael 10, 15

Rabbi Blue's Chanukkah
  Recipes 113-4
Retsina 157
Rice, Brown 37
  Stuffing 110
Riesling 157
Rioja 45, 56, 157
Rocamar 157

Salmon Sashimi 30
Salmonella bacterium 34,
  101
Samos 80
Sandwiches 87-88
Sancerre 31, 157
Sansovino 157
Saumur 157
Sausages
  Glamorgan 57
  Herbed 56
  Hereford 55
Sauternes 157
Sauvignon 31, 158
Soave 158

Soup
  Chicken and Sweetcorn
    44
  Cockie Leekie 47
  French Vegetable 12
  Pumpkin 12
  Tomato and Orange 13
Spatlese 108, 134
Stilton and Mango Toasts
  90
Stuffing, Sweet Rice with
  Saffron and Orange
  Rind 110
Syrah 159

Tafelwein 134, 159
Tavel 91
Toasted Cheese 89-90
Tomatoes
  Chutney 98
  Greek Tomato Salad 62
  Grilled, Provençal 63
  and Orange Soup 13
Trout Almondine 29
Trout en Papillote 28
Turkey 100, 101
  Norfolk 100
  Roasting, Crafty 102
  Roulade 105
Turnips Cooked with
  Tomatoes and Cumin
  Seeds 110

Valpolicella 159
Verdicchio 159
Veuve du Vernay 159-
  160
*Vino Nobile di
  Montepulciano* 135
Vouvray 160

Zinfandel 160